PRAISE FOR DARLOW

BRANDS WIN CHAMPIONSHIPS

"Die-hard fans—that one concept, that one overlooked idea—is just one of the big ideas you'll find inside this book that's not actually about sports."

—Seth Godin, author, *Linchpin*

"Win or lose, here's how to build a national reputation for your college sports brand."

—Al Ries, author, *Positioning: The Battle for Your Mind*

"A must-read for anyone in sports marketing. This book sees the future and shows you how to get there."

—Nate Scott, *USA Today Sports*, For the Win

ATHLETES ARE BRANDS TOO

"We talk to our players all the time about the importance of using social media to build their brand. The position they're in as high-profile athletes comes with great responsibility that can influence others, lift people up, and create a personal narrative. *Athletes Are Brands Too* provides a detailed guide for how athletes can begin to not only build their brand, but how to grow it, maximize it and the importance of it. In a new world where social media has become the driving force of branding, I can't think of a more effective playbook for athletes to begin building their own message."

—John Calipari, Naismith Memorial Basketball Hall of Famer

"If you are an athlete that wants to learn how to take your personal brand to the next level, then this is a must-read. Jeremy hits the nail on the head: a lot of us don't take advantage of the platform that we have to create success beyond our time in our respective sports. Personally I feel like I had plenty of knowledge in this area, but after reading this book I picked up even more of an understanding for the topic at hand. Athletes are brands too! We all have to hold each other accountable in grasping this concept so we can be free to continue living life long after our playing days are over."

—Alvin Kamara, professional football player

"In uncertain times, Jeremy Darlow maps out how to control your look, your brand, and your future. This should be a textbook for the future of interaction in sports."

—Dennis Dodd, CBS Sports senior columnist

THE DARLOW RULES

THE DARLOW RULES

75 RULES TO BECOMING AN ELITE MARKETER

JEREMY DARLOW

jack + june
publishing

Published by Jack + June Publishing

Edited and designed by Girl Friday Productions
www.girlfridayproductions.com

Editorial: Indigo
Design: Paul Barrett

Image credits: All images copyright Jeremy Darlow except page 302–303 emojis copyright Shutterstock/Cosmic_Design

ISBN: 978-0-9905622-1-4

DEDICATED TO THE:

CHALLENGERS
CROSS-EXAMINERS
DEFIERS
STRIVERS
FIGHTERS
SEEKERS
DREAMERS
ROMANTICS
MAVERICKS
DEBATERS
INSTIGATORS
RISK-TAKERS
RULE-BREAKERS

THIS BOOK IS FOR US.

CONTENTS.

Introduction 1

1. We're not as smart as we think we are. 6
2. If you're not building your brain, you're not building a brand 16
3. The world is your classroom, and everyone is a teacher 24
4. Get over yourself 32
5. Stop asking coworkers for new ideas 38
6. If you can build your brand, you can build theirs. 46
7. If you don't love the brand you're building, no one will 56
8. Don't plan for tomorrow until you know where you are today 66
9. What we see is what you get 76
10. Make a better book cover. 86
11. If you're not obsessed with building a brand, you won't 96
12. It's not about winning the day, it's about winning the decade 106
13. Know when to walk away. 112
14. Everyone's product sucks at some point 118

15. Stop lying 126
16. What makes you different is what makes you a brand 138
17. Be the only 150
18. No positioning, no differentiation, no brand 160
19. If you can't see it, you can't affect it 170
20. Focus 180
21. People follow leaders— and leaders don't follow anyone 192
22. Products serve a purpose, brands give purpose 198
23. Don't skip steps 206
24. Don't listen to an idea until you hear an objective 212
25. If it's not on paper, it's not real 220
26. Go home 228
27. There are no participation awards 234
28. Kill or be killed 242
29. You lose 100% of the fights you don't pick 250
30. Don't take the bait 258
31. Talk when they're not 266
32. Quality over quantity 272
33. Brand marketing is about empathy 278
34. Not all influence is created equal 286
35. Give your audience what they want, not what you need 292
36. It's not a brand's job to make everyone happy . . . 300
37. Kill indifference 308
38. Without hate, there is no love 314
39. Consumers are masochists 320
40. People trust people, not companies 328

41. You are the company that you keep 338
42. Influencers exist, and you need them 346
43. Fish where your fish are 352
44. Seeing is believing 360
45. Oversaturation is a good thing 366
46. Predictability builds trust 376
47. Pick one color and stick with it 384
48. Stop robbing Peter's logo to pay Paul 392
49. Once is not enough 398
50. Sometimes all you need is a base hit 406
51. There's more to marketing than social media . . . 414
52. Fake it until your brand makes it 420
53. Pull a stunt 428
54. It's easier to crash a party than throw a party . . . 436
55. Don't chase the storm, plan for it 442
56. Content is currency 448
57. No clicks, no coverage 454
58. If they're not first, they're last 460
59. Break up your stories 468
60. Flirt with your audience 474
61. People want what they're not supposed to have . 480
62. Everyone wants their fifteen minutes of fame . . . 486
63. Attach brand and PR at the hip 492
64. Don't make the logo bigger 500
65. Marketing is easy, but only if you allow it to be . 506
66. Less is always more 512
67. Big and bold is better than bold and beautiful . . 518
68. No one cares who did it first 524
69. Don't be afraid to copy, just make it better 530
70. Don't just make it better, make it yours 536
71. If you're going to say it, say it with confidence . . 542

72. Don't brand scared 552
73. Carpe diem.. 558
74. Break the rules.................................. 570
75. Rewrite the rules 578

Final Words... 582
Marketing Plan 584
Bibliography... 590
Notes... 604

MARKETING IS DYING.

Not because the industry is shrinking, but because the acumen is. Not because people are less passionate, but because people are less patient. Today's marketers are white-collar drug addicts, and their narcotics of choice are likes, retweets, and views. The cravings are real. As a result, brand strategy has become a relic, a lost art once seen as foundational knowledge for any freshly minted junior ad associate. This critical expertise has since been replaced by food emojis and generic hashtags. It's a dark time for the industry I love.

And I couldn't be more excited about it.

You see, while a new generation of marketers enters our world immediately fiending for their next hit of social currency, riding a viral high one day, and crashing back down to earth the next, you and I can soak in big-picture philosophies that produce decades of professional growth with no comedown. Whether you're a recent college graduate or a newly born-again marketer, you are holding the path to success in your hands. Let these pages set you free.

I wrote this book to teach you what I've learned over the course of my career as a marketing executive—a career that has blessed me with the opportunity to be part of some of the most successful brand launches in three highly competitive industries: video games, beer, and sports. During my time in each, invaluable lessons were passed down to me by those who came into this game in a time before cell phones, YouTube, and the need for instant gratification. I'm lucky in that way. As a professional, I've straddled the line between the days of traditional advertising and the modern world of digital marketing. I've seen the good and bad of each, combining the best of both to formulate what you will come to know as the DARLOW Rules.

This isn't my first book, but it's the most personally revealing. These truly are the secrets to my professional success. While it might be ill-advised to give years of knowledge away for the low, low price of whatever you bought this book for, it's the least I can do. After all, without the help of countless individuals who shared with me their own experiences and learnings, I wouldn't be here preaching to you.

Therein lies my first rule. Call it DARLOW Rule #0. Whether it comes from a mentor, a thought leader, or an author, seek out and collect knowledge from the people surrounding you. We are all living, breathing compilations of the professionals that came before us. The more willing we are to learn from those individuals, the more successful we'll be. That's because our industry is built on transcendent thinkers, not buzzy technologies.

Al Ries and Jack Trout literally wrote the book on brand positioning, appropriately titled *Positioning: The Battle for Your Mind*. They created a concept that remains central to every marketing plan I build today (see DARLOW Rule #18). Their work was first published in 1981. Seth Godin wrote *Purple Cow*, a brand marketing classic, and one I refer back to whenever I need a refresher on brand differentiation (see DARLOW Rule #16). That book was published in 2003. *A New Brand World*, written by Scott Bedbury, the man who taught me the importance of research (see DARLOW Rule #8), hit shelves in 2002. Each title and each person are all still critical to my success.

I don't agree with everything these legends wrote, but the principles that spoke to me then still speak to me now. I can't remember all of the pieces of wisdom my friends and colleagues have graced me with over the years, but the ones I do remember still guide me (see DARLOW Rule #72). And while I refuse to waste my time dwelling on the campaigns that failed over the course of my career, I will never forget why they failed (see DARLOW Rule #13). Put all of those experiences together, and you have *The DARLOW Rules*.

This book is a marketing mixtape made up of my favorite philosophies, lessons, failures, and triumphs. These concepts are not unique to me; only the collection is. My experiences in work and life do not and will not match anyone else's, and for that reason, no two marketers or rule books are the same. That's where you come in. As you read, the mission is simple: trash the rules you hate, steal the rules you love, and build from there.

■

Before you dive in, I need to give you some instructions on how to properly read this book (yes, I'm serious). First, grab a pen and a highlighter. Do not enter into this experience without one of each. I'll reiterate this again later, but *The DARLOW Rules* is as much a workbook as it is something to simply digest.

Second, do not binge-read the material. This isn't Netflix. I want you to sit with each rule and truly engage. Underline, scribble, and paint on the forthcoming pages with your own thoughts and feelings. One rule at a time. Each rule has its close cousins, but like marketers, no two rules are exactly alike. Get to know each for what it is and how it can help you before moving on to the next.

Which leads me to directive number three. Do not treat *The DARLOW Rules* as a one-time read; instead, plan to come back to the book every three to six months to track your brand's progress. Following each rule, you will find a homework section. I'll ask you to answer the same questions and complete the same tasks I myself complete when building a marketing plan. However, as is the case with any brand, a marketing plan is always changing. Your answers today may not look the same tomorrow, but that's the point. Your brand will evolve, and as it does, so too should your analysis.

Finally, you don't need to agree with everything I say, but you do need to have an open mind for this to work. I can't help you unless you accept that you need help. Just because you checked into the treatment facility doesn't mean you're cured. We have work to do.

LET'S GET STARTED.

WE'RE NOT AS SMART AS WE THINK WE ARE

RULE #1

I'm not as smart as I think I am, and if you're honest with yourself, neither are you. But in my experience, that's a good thing. At least it can be, if you recognize it and embrace it. Now, I will admit that in the beginning, that's not easy. Like many, I came out of school thinking I had all of the answers. I was wrong. It took a marketing veteran to wake me up.

It was early in my days working for the video game company Ubisoft as an associate brand manager. I knew I had the instinct to be a great marketer; what I didn't know was that instinct is only part of the battle. One morning, my eventual mentor approached with a game in his hand. He dropped it on my desk, saying, "This is your game now. Build a plan." Wait, what? My professional life flashed before my eyes. I had no idea what to do. It turned out that I didn't have all of the answers. But I was saved by someone who did—my mentor.

He waited until later that day, as if testing my resilience, to return with the solution in hand, this time in the form of a PowerPoint template. It walked me through, step by step, how to build a marketing plan. He had provided a map to a lost marketer. It changed my life and career. It became clear that building a brand had less to do with instinct and more to do with the planning process itself.

I've used my own version of that map ever since. I can honestly say I wouldn't be where I am today without that experience and without my mentor. I take nothing for granted. I know I'm not as good as I think I am, but that's why I've had success. It's the reason I work harder, read more, and strive to be better than my competition.

The truth is, **we're not as smart as we think we are**, but that's a good thing—if we allow it to be.

TEACH THY TONGUE TO SAY,

'I DO NOT KNOW,'

AND THOU SHALT PROGRESS."

—MAIMONIDES

HOMEWORK

DATE ....

As a marketer, what areas do you need to improve on?

What steps are you taking today to get better?

What steps can you take tomorrow to get better?

Who in your life can act as a professional mentor?

HOMEWORK+3

Three months after you've completed your initial homework assignment on the preceding pages, come back to this rule and answer the following questions to reflect your brand's current state.

DATE ....

As a marketer, what areas do you need to improve on?

What steps are you taking today to get better?

What steps can you take tomorrow to get better?

Who in your life can act as a professional mentor?

HOMEWORK+6

Six months after you've completed your HOMEWORK+3 assignment on the preceding pages, come back to this rule and fill out the below to reflect your brand's current state.

DATE ....

As a marketer, what areas do you need to improve on?

What steps are you taking today to get better?

What steps can you take tomorrow to get better?

Who in your life can act as a professional mentor?

IF YOU'RE NOT BUILDING YOUR BRAIN, YOU'RE NOT BUILDING A BRAND

RULE #2

The road maps to marketing success can be found in a bookstore near you. Yet according to a 2018 Pew Research Center survey, 24% of American adults had failed to read any part of a book during the prior year. As a marketer, I find this to be a particularly troubling stat. How can we expect to improve the brands we manage if we refuse to improve ourselves? **If you're not building your brain, you're not building a brand.** Bottom line. Learning from the writings of those who came before (and after) me has been a critical part of my success. I'm not the marketer I am today without the literary assistance of the industry's most brilliant minds.

But don't just read, engage. Take notes. Write in the margins. Highlight key points. Marketing books are journals, not pieces of fine china. Use and abuse them. The more you put into a book, the more your career will get out of it.

Aspiring marketers will often ask me, "What do I need to do to get to where you are?" The answer is always the same: read.

A lot.

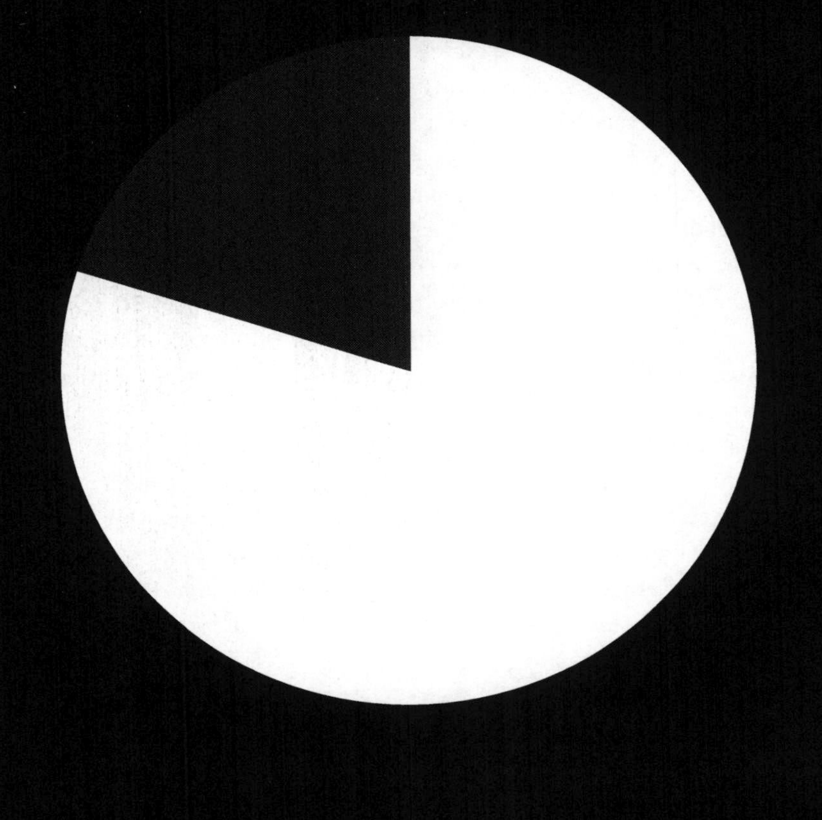

80%

ACCORDING TO AN ARTICLE IN *BUSINESS INSIDER*, RENOWNED INVESTOR WARREN BUFFETT "SPENDS ABOUT 80% OF HIS DAY READING." PER *USA TODAY*, WHEN ASKED ABOUT THE KEY TO SUCCESS, THE BILLIONAIRE POINTED TO A STACK OF NEARBY BOOKS AND SAID, "READ 500 PAGES LIKE THIS EVERY DAY. THAT'S HOW KNOWLEDGE WORKS. IT BUILDS UP, LIKE COMPOUND INTEREST. ALL OF YOU CAN DO IT, BUT I GUARANTEE NOT MANY OF YOU WILL DO IT."

PROVE HIM WRONG.

HOMEWORK

Pick one marketing or business-related book per month to read over the course of the next year, and fill in your choices below.

After you read each title, list the brand marketing rules presented in that particular book that you plan to incorporate in your own work:

JANUARY ....

RULES ....

....

FEBRUARY ....

RULES ....

....

MARCH ....

RULES ....

....

APRIL ....

RULES ....

....

MAY ....

RULES ....

....

JUNE ....

RULES ....

....

JULY ....

RULES ....

....

AUGUST ....

RULES ....

....

SEPTEMBER ....

RULES ....

....

OCTOBER ....

RULES ....

....

NOVEMBER ....

RULES ....

....

DECEMBER ....

RULES ....

....

"EDUCATION COSTS MONEY. BUT THEN SO DOES IGNORANCE."

—SIR CLAUS MOSER

THE WORLD IS YOUR CLASS-ROOM, AND EVERY-ONE IS A TEACHER

RULE #3

As professionals, we often fail to pick up on the nontypical marketing lessons that surround us on a daily basis. The truth is, there are few elements in life that are void of promotion. Everyone's in the business of selling himself or herself or this product or that service. Some you love and some you hate, but in all cases there's education to be had.

You're not a fan of Miley Cyrus? No problem, but don't overlook the incredible presence she's built among young female fans. Learn from her. Not into the WWE? That's fine, but realize, despite your aversion to it, that the wrestling entertainment giant has developed more influential personalities from scratch than perhaps any other organization in the world. Learn from it. Sick of hearing about the Kardashians? Sure, they can dominate your television, your social feed, and your water cooler conversation at work, but that's why you should care. Learn from them. It's those who take the time to understand the nuance of the brand successes and failures around us who will develop as marketers and ultimately build strong brands.

The world is your classroom, and everyone is a teacher.

"WHAT WE HAVE LEARNED FROM OTHERS BECOMES OUR OWN BY REFLECTION."

—RALPH WALDO EMERSON

HOMEWORK

DATE ....

Make a list of five popular musicians or bands that you dislike.

....
....
....
....
....
....
....
....
....
....

Write down reasons why, despite your aversion, these performers have gained notoriety.

....
....
....
....
....
....
....
....
....
....

What lessons from your list of reasons can you apply to your brand?

HOMEWORK+3

Three months after you've completed your initial homework assignment on the preceding pages, come back to this rule and fill out the below to reflect your brand's current state.

DATE ....

Make a list of five popular actors or actresses that you dislike.

....

....

....

....

....

Write down reasons why, despite your aversion, these performers have gained notoriety.

What lessons from your list of reasons can you apply to your brand?

GET OVER YOUR-SELF

RULE #4

The less self-righteousness you have in your professional life, the stronger your professional career will be. I'm not saying do things you know to be immoral and wrong—quite the opposite. What I am saying is that a mind free of judgment is a mind free to learn, even from those you may not agree with. Some of the most debated characters in our history happen to be some of the most instructive brands. Show me a president of the United States that you believe to have failed at the job of commander-in-chief, and I'll show you a personal brand you can learn from—but only if you allow yourself to see past your own conceit to reveal the true marketing lesson.

Before you step another foot into that office, kill your ego, embrace humility, and **get over yourself**. You'll be a better marketer for it.

SELF-ENHANCEMENT EFFECT:

ACCORDING TO *SCIENTIFIC AMERICAN*, "WHEN COMPARING OURSELVES VERSUS OTHER PEOPLE, WE TEND TO RATE OURSELVES MORE HIGHLY ON A HOST OF POSITIVE MEASURES, INCLUDING INTELLIGENCE, AMBITION, FRIENDLINESS, AND MODESTY. . . . THIS FINDING IS SOMETIMES CALLED THE 'SELF-ENHANCEMENT EFFECT.'"

ALSO KNOWN AS THE REASON SOME PEOPLE FAIL TO IMPROVE.

HOMEWORK

In your estimation, why did people vote for the current leader of your home country?

....

....

....

....

....

....

....

....

....

....

....

From a marketing perspective, what did this individual do well in his or her campaign?

....

....

....

....

....

....

....

....

....

....

....

From a marketing perspective, what did the challenger fail to do in his or her campaign?

What lessons can you take from each and apply to your brand?

STOP ASKING CO-WORKERS FOR NEW IDEAS

RULE #5

You want to know how to generate headlines for your brand? Ask the media what they need in order to write a compelling story. Crazy, right? As obvious as that might sound, it's exceedingly rare to find organizations, and even industries, that actively seek outside opinions. I once attended a conference focused on ways to obtain media coverage, and the thing that astonished me about this particular event was the surprising lack of journalists brought in to speak. And by "lack of journalists," I mean no journalists. Who better to sit down and discuss media strategy with than the folks actually writing the stories?

We spend all day in our offices bouncing ideas around with individuals who have similar jobs, similar experiences, and similar ways of thinking. Why then would we attend a conference populated with that same breed of like-minded humans, the only difference being the company logos they wear on their polos? It makes no sense.

If you want to learn something new, get out of your bubble. Seek out unorthodox ways of thinking. And please, *please* **stop asking coworkers for new ideas**. They don't have any.

ECHO CHAMBER:

"AN ENVIRONMENT IN WHICH A PERSON ENCOUNTERS ONLY BELIEFS OR OPINIONS THAT COINCIDE WITH THEIR OWN, SO THAT THEIR EXISTING VIEWS ARE REINFORCED AND ALTERNATIVE IDEAS ARE NOT CONSIDERED." (GOOGLE DEFINITIONS)

HARD TO INNOVATE FROM INSIDE AN ECHO CHAMBER.

HOMEWORK

Write down your five favorite consumer brands (outside of the industry you work in).

....

....

....

....

....

....

....

....

....

....

....

....

....

....

....

....

From this group, list three of your favorite advertising campaigns and what you like about each.

CAMPAIGN ....

WHY? ....

WHY? ....

WHY? ....

CAMPAIGN ....
WHY? ....
WHY? ....
WHY? ....

CAMPAIGN ....
WHY? ....
WHY? ....
WHY? ....

What lessons from your list can you apply to your brand?

....
....
....
....
....
....
....
....
....
....
....
....
....
....
....
....
....
....
....

"ODD THAT WE DON'T SOLICIT A SECOND OPINION FROM DOCTORS AFTER RECEIVING A GOOD MEDICAL DIAGNOSIS."

—NEIL DEGRASSE TYSON

IF YOU CAN BUILD YOUR BRAND, YOU CAN'T BUILD THEIRS

RULE #6

If you don't have a strong personal brand of your own, what makes you think you can build ours? That's what executives should be asking potential marketing candidates. You are your own brand, and your ability to build individual notoriety is a surefire way to prove your skill set to the company you want to work for. Not only that, it's a reliable means to sharpening your sword.

But it's not easy.

I can tell you from experience that building a personal brand, versus that of a corporation, is much more difficult. If that advertising campaign doesn't pan out, it's not your money lost, it's the company's. And they can handle it. On the other hand, when you spend a year of your life on a project meant to build awareness around your own brand and it doesn't work, you're in a hole that many people fail to climb back out of.

The experience and resilience that comes from building a personal brand is invaluable to you and your future employer. By finding success on your own, you not only become a better marketer, you become a better candidate, proving that **if you can build your brand, you can build theirs**.

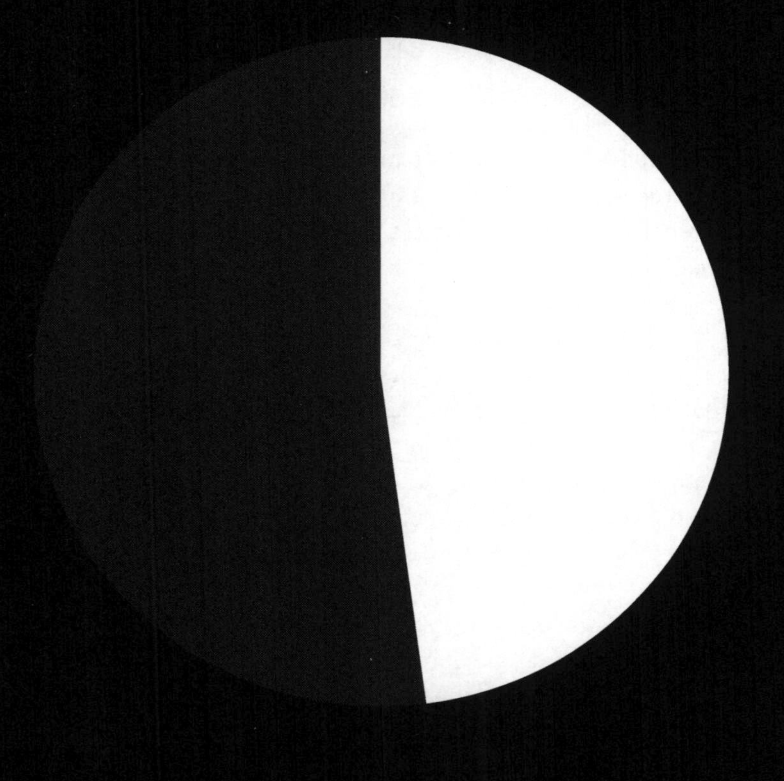

48%

ACCORDING TO A HARRIS INTERACTIVE SURVEY, 75% OF PARTICIPANTS SAID THEY HAVE GOOGLED THEMSELVES IN THE PAST. FROM THAT GROUP, 48% REPORTED THAT THE RESULTS WERE NOT POSITIVE, WHILE 30% FOUND THAT NOTHING OF RELEVANCE CAME UP, AND 13% SAID THEY WOULD "CHANGE THE RESULTS TO BETTER REFLECT WHO THEY ARE."

YOU ARE YOUR OWN BRAND MANAGER. IF YOU DON'T LIKE WHAT YOU SEE, CHANGE IT.

HOMEWORK

DATE ....

What makes your personal brand different from your professional competition?

....

....

....

....

....

....

....

....

....

....

What are you doing beyond your day job to differentiate yourself today?

....

....

....

....

....

....

....

....

....

....

What more can you do to differentiate yourself tomorrow?

Do you have a personal brand marketing plan?

YES: Use the question and activity sections in this book to continue refining your plan.
NO: Use the question and activity sections in this book to start building a plan.

HOMEWORK+3

Three months after you've completed your initial homework assignment on the preceding pages, come back to this rule and fill out the below to reflect your personal brand's current state.

DATE ....

What makes your personal brand different from that of your professional competition?

What are you doing beyond your day job to differentiate yourself?

What more can you do outside of your day job to differentiate yourself?

HOMEWORK+6

Six months after you've completed your HOMEWORK+3 assignment on the preceding pages, come back to this rule and fill out the below to reflect your personal brand's current state.

DATE ....

What makes your personal brand different from that of your professional competition?

....
....
....
....
....
....
....
....
....
....
....
....
....
....
....
....
....
....
....

What are you doing beyond your day job to differentiate yourself?

....

....

....

....

....

....

....

....

....

....

....

....

....

What more can you do outside of your day job to differentiate yourself?

....

....

....

....

....

....

....

....

....

....

....

....

....

IF YOU DON'T LOVE THE BRAND YOU'RE BUILDING, NO ONE WILL

RULE #7

They say you have to love yourself before anyone else will. I've seen that same thinking hold true in brand marketing. **If you don't love the brand you're building, no one will.** Show us you care, show us it matters, and show us it's not about the money. Only then will we show you the love you need to attain market leadership.

Brands that exude genuine passion breed genuine passion. According to the *Harvard Business Review*, that matters in leadership: "Passions are the deep internal drivers of behavior that distinguish good leaders from great ones." Leaders like former PepsiCo CEO and Yale University graduate Indra Nooyi, who, according to *The Guardian*, "worked as a receptionist from midnight to 5 am to help pay for her tuition." That's passion. Leaders like Dallas Mavericks owner Mark Cuban, who waited seven years before taking a vacation while building his first company. That's passion. And leaders like Martin Luther King Jr., whose fight for civil rights drove hundreds of thousands of people to march on Washington. That's passion.

Before you decide to embark on your own brand journey, look in the mirror. Does the brand you're building come from the heart, or is it driven by the wallet? The former will work, the latter won't.

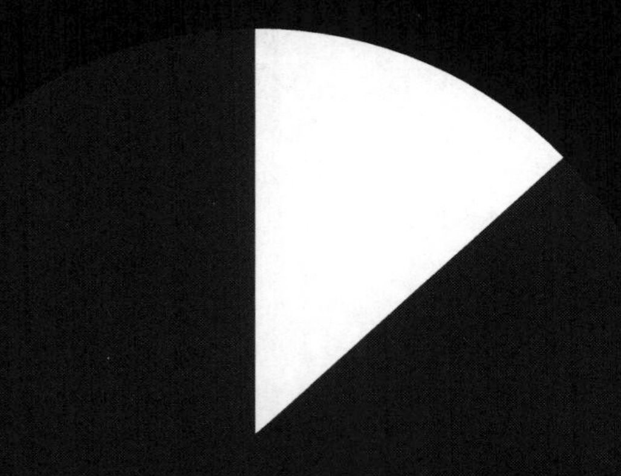

13%

ACCORDING TO A STUDY BY DELOITTE'S CENTER FOR THE EDGE, JUST 13% OF THE UNITED STATES WORKFORCE IS PASSIONATE ABOUT THEIR JOBS. THAT FORMULA IS INCOMPATIBLE WITH BRAND DEVELOPMENT. IF YOU LOVE IT, YOU CAN BUILD A BRAND AROUND IT. IF YOU DON'T LOVE IT, MOVE ON.

HOMEWORK

What are you personally passionate about?

Does the brand you are building today fit into any of your answers? If not, go build a brand that does.

HOMEWORK

List your favorite parts of the brand you're building.

Rank them in order, from most beloved to least beloved.

Focus on developing the part of your brand that you love the most.

List the types of people or communities who would be most attracted to the part of your brand you ranked number one overall.

Rank these groups in order from most passionate to least passionate.

Focus your efforts on connecting with the group you ranked number one overall.

“IF YOU LOVE IT, IF YOU HAVE A PASSION FOR IT, THEN KEEP DOING IT.”

—MEGAN RAPINOE

DON'T PLAN FOR TOMORROW UNTIL YOU KNOW WHERE YOU ARE TODAY

RULE #8

Did you know it's impossible for Google Maps to deliver directions without first knowing your current location? Don't believe me? Pull up the application on your phone, input your desired destination, leave the starting point field blank, and see what happens. Nothing. Nothing happens. Even the all-knowing Google can't tell you how to get somewhere without first knowing where you are right now (. . . wait for the brand marketing connection . . .).

Similarly, before you start thinking about where you want to take your brand, you must first pinpoint where it sits currently. That leads us to step one of any successful marketing plan: research. A *lot* of research—what I call the situation analysis. In this initial planning phase, it's your job to lift every rock and look under every hood to determine where your brand fits, what makes it different, and how you can create an impact in the marketplace. **Don't plan for tomorrow until you know where you are today.**

Fair warning: this is the most tedious and time-consuming portion of the planning process. But there's good news: not only will your analysis identify your current location, but it will also set you on a path to determining your brand's appropriate final destination. Once you know where you're starting from and where you ultimately want to go, drawing a map to get you there is easy.

So easy, even Google could do it.

Draw a path from your current location (*point A*) to your desired destination (*point B*).

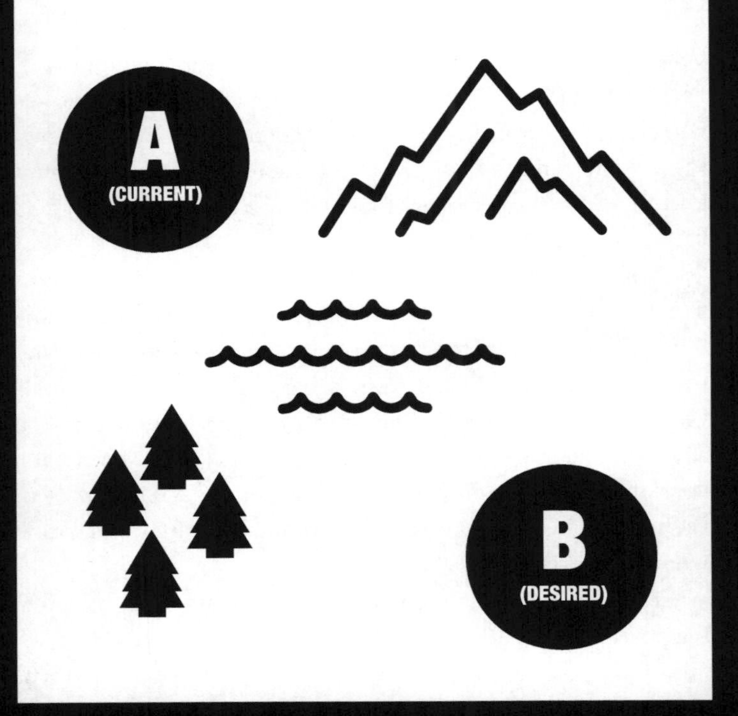

PRETTY EASY, RIGHT? LET'S TRY AGAIN.

Draw a path from your current location to your desired destination (*point B*).
B
(DESIRED)

CAN'T DO IT, CAN YOU? THAT'S BECAUSE IT'S IMPOSSIBLE TO OUTLINE A PATH TO A DESIRED DESTINATION WITHOUT FIRST IDENTIFYING YOUR CURRENT LOCATION. ANY ATTEMPT TO DO SO IS NOTHING MORE THAN A GUESS.

HOMEWORK

DATE ....

SWOT ANALYSIS

STRENGTHS: Make a list of your brand's strengths.

WEAKNESSES: Make a list of your brand's weaknesses.

OPPORTUNITIES: Make a list of industry opportunities your brand can capitalize on.

THREATS: Make a list of advantages the competition has over your brand.

Don't pull any punches. The more critical you are in evaluating your brand today, the better equipped you will be to improve it tomorrow. As you make your way through the forthcoming rules and corresponding homework assignments (each of which will contribute to your situation analysis), you will undoubtedly uncover new strengths, weaknesses, opportunities, and threats that are different from those you've listed here. As each supplementary point is revealed, return to this rule and add it to your SWOT analysis.

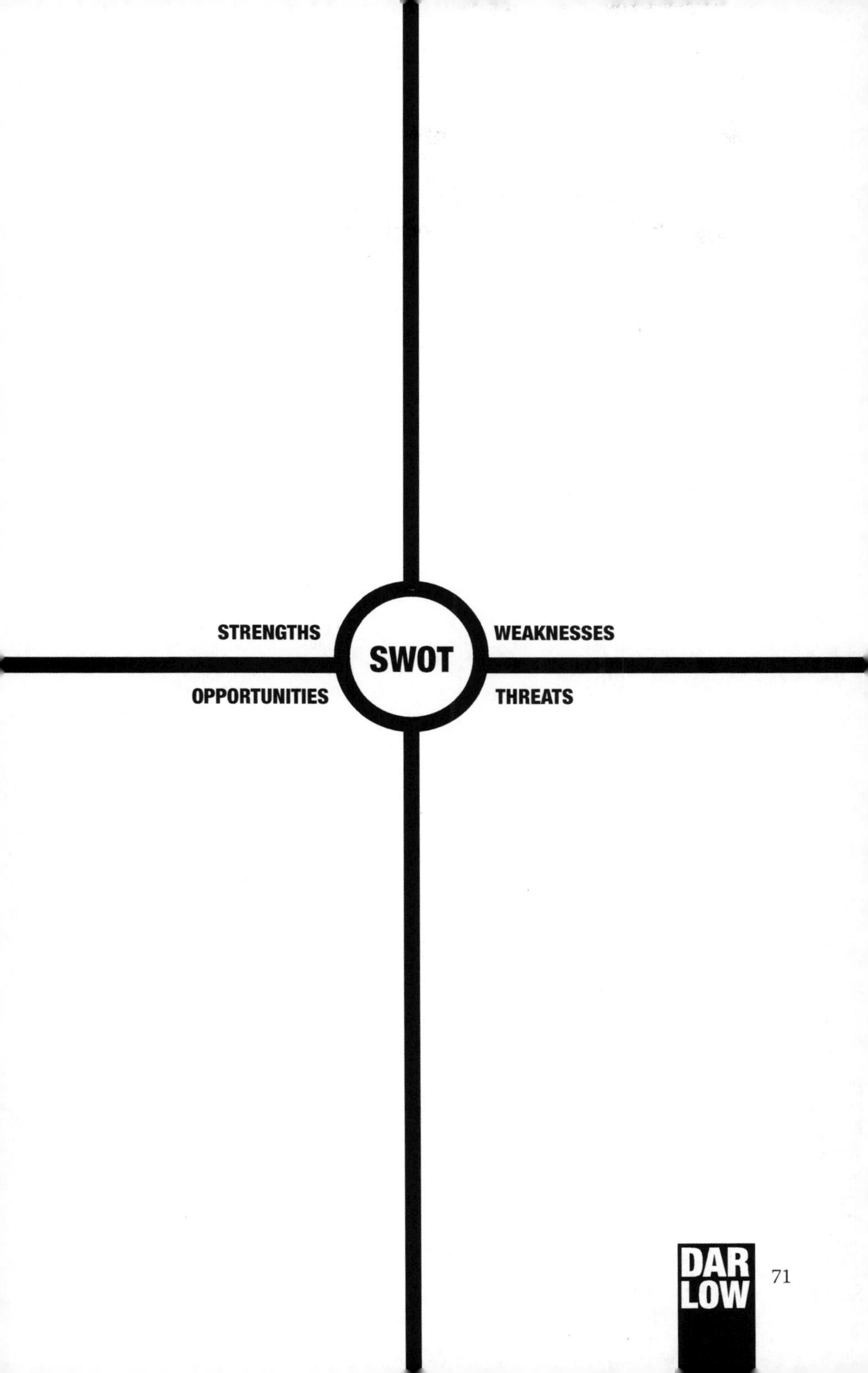

STRENGTHS

WEAKNESSES

SWOT

OPPORTUNITIES

THREATS

HOMEWORK+3

Three months after you've completed your initial homework assignment on the preceding pages, come back to this rule and fill out the following page to reflect your brand's current state.

DATE ....

SWOT ANALYSIS

STRENGTHS: Make a list of your brand's strengths.

WEAKNESSES: Make a list of your brand's weaknesses.

OPPORTUNITIES: Make a list of industry opportunities your brand can capitalize on.

THREATS: Make a list of advantages the competition has over your brand.

STRENGTHS

WEAKNESSES

SWOT

OPPORTUNITIES

THREATS

HOMEWORK+6

Six months after you've completed your HOMEWORK+3 assignment on the preceding pages, come back to this rule and fill out the following page to reflect your brand's current state.

DATE ....

SWOT ANALYSIS

STRENGTHS: Make a list of your brand's strengths.

WEAKNESSES: Make a list of your brand's weaknesses.

OPPORTUNITIES: Make a list of industry opportunities your brand can capitalize on.

THREATS: Make a list of advantages the competition has over your brand.

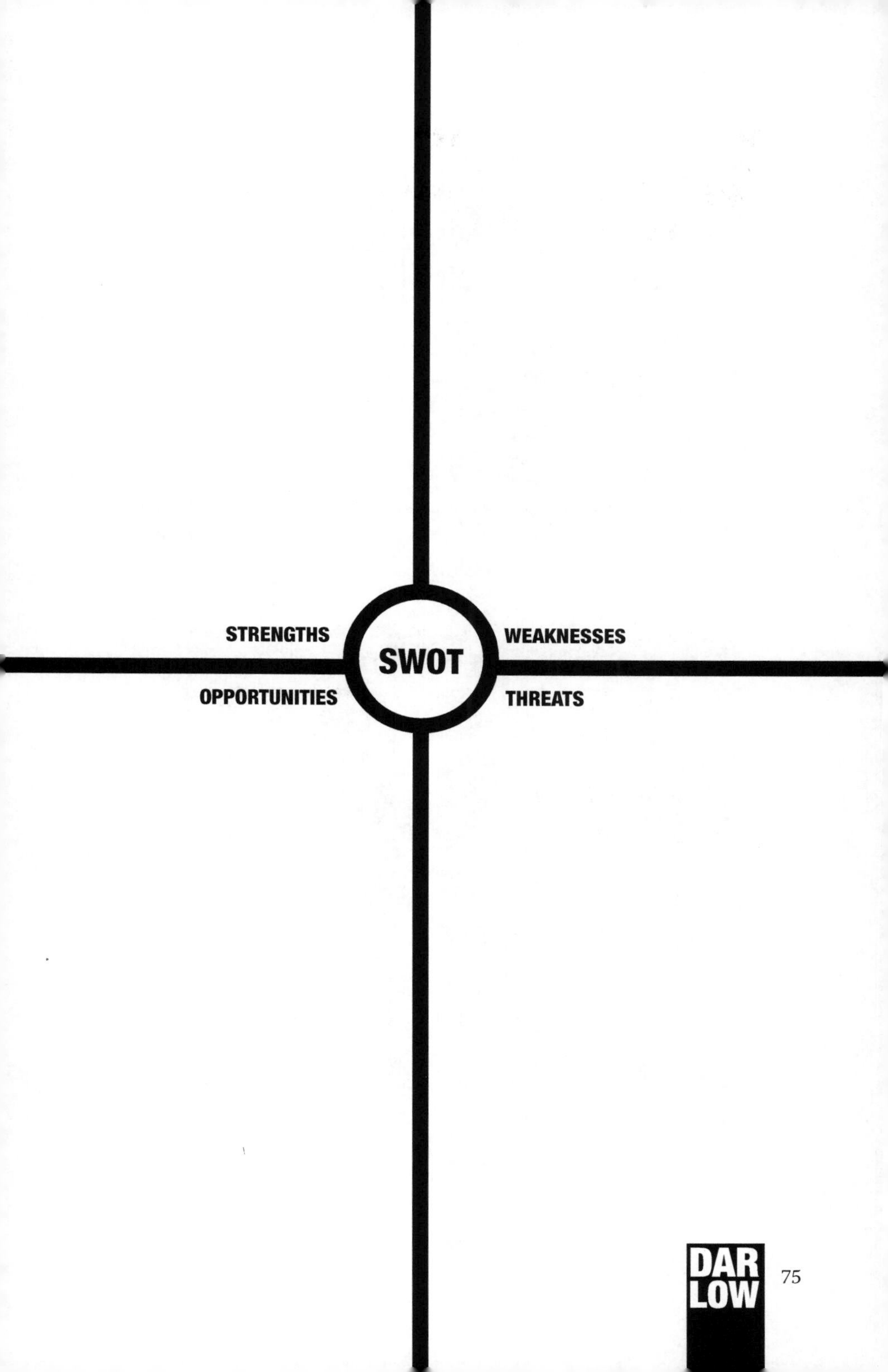

STRENGTHS

WEAKNESSES

SWOT

OPPORTUNITIES

THREATS

DAR
LOW

WHAT WE SEE IS WHAT YOU GET

RULE #9

Would it surprise you to hear that the average college student is twenty years old? No? Okay, what if I told you that at just six foot seven, Dennis Rodman ranks in the top five for total rebounds in NBA history? Too obvious? How about this one: on average, men think about sex every seven seconds. Still not shocked?

Well, you should be on all accounts. The average college student is twenty-six years old, Dennis Rodman sits outside of the top twenty in all-time rebounding, and the closest thing to actual fact suggests that men think of sex at least once a day, not every seven seconds. So why is it that few people flinch when hearing these aforementioned statements?

Perception.

What we're fed on television, in the news, and through peer-to-peer storytelling is a depiction of a beautiful early twentysomething college student, a bright-haired basketball player who never missed a rebound, and a gender obsessed with sex. Influencing minds at a mass level is that easy. Present one idea over and over again from a variety of touchpoints, and eventually it becomes true. Human opinions are malleable. Which means no matter where your brand is today, tomorrow can be a new, more profitable era.

You may not have the best-selling basketball shoe in the sport right now, but get a group of influential people talking about it, the most-beloved players wearing it, and the biggest blogs writing about it, and soon it will seem like you do. That's how perception works.

What we see is what you get.

"REALITY LEAVES A LOT TO THE IMAGINATION."

—JOHN LENNON

HOMEWORK

DATE ....

What is the perception of your brand today?

What do people say about you in public forums?

What do your friends and family think of your brand?

....

....

....

....

....

....

....

....

....

....

....

Are you happy with your brand's perception today? Why or why not?

....

....

....

....

....

....

....

....

....

....

....

Whether or not it's accurate to you, what people think and say about your brand is the truth to them. And that's all that matters.

HOMEWORK+3

Three months after you've completed your initial homework assignment on the preceding pages, come back to this rule and fill out the below to reflect your brand's current state.

DATE ....

What is the perception of your brand today?

What do people say about you in public forums?

What do your friends and family think of your brand?

....

....

....

....

....

....

....

....

....

....

....

....

....

Are you happy with your brand's perception today? Why or why not?

....

....

....

....

....

....

....

....

....

....

....

....

....

....

HOMEWORK+6

Six months after you've completed your HOMEWORK+3 assignment on the preceding pages, come back to this rule and fill out the below to reflect your brand's current state.

DATE ....

What is the perception of your brand today?

....

....

....

....

....

....

....

....

....

What do people say about you in public forums?

....

....

....

....

....

....

....

....

....

What do your friends and family think of your brand?

Are you happy with your brand's perception today? Why or why not?

MAKE A BETTER BOOK COVER

RULE #10

We judge books by their covers, and we always will. Is it right? Perhaps not. Can we change it? Definitely not. We're human and we're shallow. No one is free from judging; likewise, no one is free from judgment. And thanks to the unrealistic expectations being served up by social media, it's only going to get worse. Yet underneath it all, a critical brand marketing lesson can be found.

Rather than fighting the inevitability of scrutiny, just **make a better book cover**. Judgment is driven by perception, and, as I noted in the previous rule, perception is malleable. What people think or say about your brand is completely up to you; you're the one pulling the strings, not the consumer. How you portray your brand will be directly reflected back to you, so you better make it (look) good.

The nightclub with the long line out front is *perceived* to be more popular and cooler than the competitor across the street sans line. That was planned. The reality is the club with a wait is often empty inside. The sneaker that sells out in minutes, to the dismay of thousands of customers who didn't get there in time, is *perceived* to be cooler than the shoe readily available online and in stores. That was planned. The reality is the shoe was purposely limited to begin with. Strings pulled. Covers designed. Perceptions changed.

Brands built.

WHICH DO YOU THINK HAS THE BETTER PIZZA?

THE MORE CONSUMERS YOU HAVE WAITING IN LINE TO GET IN AND ENGAGE WITH YOUR PRODUCT, THE MORE PEOPLE WATCHING FROM AFAR WILL ASSUME WHAT YOU'RE SELLING IS WORTH THEIR OWN TIME AND MONEY.

HOMEWORK

DATE ....

What areas of your brand have the greatest effect on its perception?

PERCEPTION DRIVER ....
PERCEPTION DRIVER ....
PERCEPTION DRIVER ....
PERCEPTION DRIVER ....
PERCEPTION DRIVER ....
PERCEPTION DRIVER ....
PERCEPTION DRIVER ....
PERCEPTION DRIVER ....

What changes can you make in those areas today to improve upon or correct your perception tomorrow?

PERCEPTION DRIVER ....
CHANGE ....
CHANGE ....
CHANGE ....

PERCEPTION DRIVER ....
CHANGE ....
CHANGE ....
CHANGE ....

PERCEPTION DRIVER ....
CHANGE ....
CHANGE ....
CHANGE ....

PERCEPTION DRIVER ....
CHANGE ....
CHANGE ....
CHANGE ....

PERCEPTION DRIVER ....
CHANGE ....
CHANGE ....
CHANGE ....

PERCEPTION DRIVER ....
CHANGE ....
CHANGE ....
CHANGE ....

PERCEPTION DRIVER ....
CHANGE ....
CHANGE ....
CHANGE ....

PERCEPTION DRIVER ....
CHANGE ....
CHANGE ....
CHANGE ....

HOMEWORK+3

Three months after you've completed your initial homework assignment on the preceding pages, come back to this rule and fill out the below to reflect your brand's current state.

DATE ....

What areas of your brand have the greatest effect on its perception?

PERCEPTION DRIVER ....
PERCEPTION DRIVER ....
PERCEPTION DRIVER ....
PERCEPTION DRIVER ....
PERCEPTION DRIVER ....
PERCEPTION DRIVER ....
PERCEPTION DRIVER ....

What changes can you make in those areas today to improve upon or correct your perception tomorrow?

PERCEPTION DRIVER ....
CHANGE ....
CHANGE ....
CHANGE ....

PERCEPTION DRIVER ....
CHANGE ....
CHANGE ....
CHANGE ....

PERCEPTION DRIVER ....
CHANGE ....
CHANGE ....
CHANGE ....

PERCEPTION DRIVER ....
CHANGE ....
CHANGE ....
CHANGE ....

PERCEPTION DRIVER ....
CHANGE ....
CHANGE ....
CHANGE ....

PERCEPTION DRIVER ....
CHANGE ....
CHANGE ....
CHANGE ....

PERCEPTION DRIVER ....
CHANGE ....
CHANGE ....
CHANGE ....

HOMEWORK+6

Six months after you've completed your HOMEWORK+3 assignment on the preceding pages, come back to this rule and fill out the below to reflect your brand's current state.

DATE ....

What areas of your brand have the greatest effect on its perception?

PERCEPTION DRIVER ....
PERCEPTION DRIVER ....
PERCEPTION DRIVER ....
PERCEPTION DRIVER ....
PERCEPTION DRIVER ....
PERCEPTION DRIVER ....
PERCEPTION DRIVER ....

What changes can you make in those areas today to improve upon or correct your perception tomorrow?

PERCEPTION DRIVER ....
CHANGE ....
CHANGE ....
CHANGE ....

PERCEPTION DRIVER ....
CHANGE ....
CHANGE ....
CHANGE ....

PERCEPTION DRIVER ....
CHANGE ....
CHANGE ....
CHANGE ....

PERCEPTION DRIVER ....
CHANGE ....
CHANGE ....
CHANGE ....

PERCEPTION DRIVER ....
CHANGE ....
CHANGE ....
CHANGE ....

PERCEPTION DRIVER ....
CHANGE ....
CHANGE ....
CHANGE ....

PERCEPTION DRIVER ....
CHANGE ....
CHANGE ....
CHANGE ....

IF YOU'RE NOT OBSESSED WITH BUILDING A BRAND, YOU WON'T

RULE #11

Great marketers never take their foot off the gas. Great marketers never pause to read their press clippings. And great marketers never pat themselves on the back for a job well done. The job, in fact, is never done. Successful professionals in our industry quietly take the learnings from one project and translate them into improvements on the next. And in that, you will find the lesson.

If you're not obsessed with building a brand, you won't. The key to a prosperous career in our world is a relentless pursuit of progress. One can never stop looking for cracks in what may appear to be flawless armor. Where is the brand susceptible? Where are the holes? How can it grow? Improve. Improve. Improve.

The ability to self-critique one's own work without flinching is the key to victory. If you're expecting anything else, this isn't the industry for you. Is that harsh? Yes, but so is the real world. Is it easy to work like this? No, but like they say, nothing worth your time ever is.

“

THE

RIGHT

WAY

IS THE

HARD

WAY.

”

—JERRY SEINFELD

HOMEWORK

DATE ....

Review the messaging, advertising, and content your brand has pushed out to the public in the past six months.

Is there a consistent brand message?

YES ....

NAME IT IN ONE SENTENCE. ....

NO ....

WHAT COULD IT BE? ....

Is there a clear consumer takeaway as to what makes your brand different?

YES ....

NAME IT IN ONE SENTENCE. ....

NO ....

WHAT COULD IT BE? ....

Is there a consistent voice and tone?

YES ....
DESCRIBE IT IN ONE SENTENCE. ....

NO ....
WHAT COULD IT BE? ....

Is there a consistent visual look and feel?

YES ....
DESCRIBE IT IN ONE SENTENCE. ....

NO ....
WHAT COULD IT BE? ....

HOMEWORK+3

Three months after you've completed your initial homework assignment on the preceding pages, come back to this rule and fill out the below to reflect your brand's current state.

DATE ....

Review the messaging, advertising, and content your brand has pushed out to the public in the past three months.

Is there a consistent brand message?

YES ....
NAME IT IN ONE SENTENCE. ....

NO ....
WHAT COULD IT BE? ....

Is there a clear consumer takeaway as to what makes your brand different?

YES ....
NAME IT IN ONE SENTENCE. ....

NO ....
WHAT COULD IT BE? ....

Is there a consistent voice and tone?

YES ....

DESCRIBE IT IN ONE SENTENCE. ....

NO ....

WHAT COULD IT BE? ....

Is there a consistent visual look and feel?

YES ....

DESCRIBE IT IN ONE SENTENCE. ....

NO ....

WHAT COULD IT BE? ....

HOMEWORK+6

Six months after you've completed your HOMEWORK+3 assignment on the preceding pages, come back to this rule and fill out the below to reflect your brand's current state.

DATE ....

Review the messaging, advertising, and content your brand has pushed out to the public in the past six months.

Is there a consistent brand message?

YES ....
NAME IT IN ONE SENTENCE. ....

NO ....
WHAT COULD IT BE? ....

Is there a clear consumer takeaway as to what makes your brand different?

YES ....
NAME IT IN ONE SENTENCE. ....

NO ....
WHAT COULD IT BE? ....

Is there a consistent voice and tone?

YES ....

DESCRIBE IT IN ONE SENTENCE. ....

NO ....

WHAT COULD IT BE? ....

Is there a consistent visual look and feel?

YES ....

DESCRIBE IT IN ONE SENTENCE. ....

NO ....

WHAT COULD IT BE? ....

IT'S NOT ABOUT WINNING THE DAY, IT'S ABOUT WINNING THE DECADE

RULE #12

Brand marketing is not about today. It's not about tomorrow. It's not even about next year. Brand marketing is about the next ten years. The old cliché "It's a marathon, not a sprint" is the shoe that fits our industry best. It takes years to build a sustainable brand that people care about. Yet despite that, the natural inclination of marketers is to sprint out of the gates.

But just like that Olympic marathoner who charges to a huge lead, fooling all of us into thinking he or she has the gold medal locked up, brands that redline early can't sustain their pace and eventually run out of gas. Slow and steady may not be the sexiest way to build a brand or run a race, but it works.

Before you rush to share tomorrow's plan with me, tell me about your goals for the week. Before you tell me about your goals for the week, show me your goals for the month. Before you show me your goals for the month—you guessed it—walk me through your goals for the year. Even before all of that, begin by presenting your plan for the next ten years. Because as a brand marketer, **it's not about winning the day, it's about winning the decade.**

"SOMEONE'S SITTING IN THE SHADE TODAY

BECAUSE SOMEONE PLANTED A TREE A LONG TIME AGO."

—WARREN BUFFETT

HOMEWORK

Describe where you want your brand to be in five years.

Ten years . . .

Twenty years . . .

What are you doing today to get there?

The more effort you put in now, the stronger your brand can be tomorrow.

KNOW WHEN TO WALK AWAY

RULE #13

If you've ever ended a romantic relationship, you can relate to the old adage "Breaking up is hard to do." Even when severing ties is clearly the best option, it's never easy. As marketers, we often find ourselves on the same emotional roller coaster while building bonds with the projects we work on and the brands we manage.

At one point, I got stuck on this ride while developing video content for an upcoming product launch. The concept was meant to feature a prominent comedian to host the video while incorporating two of our most well-known brand advocates.

But as is often the case, things did not go according to plan. The A-list comedians were out of our price range, the B-list names didn't excite us, and the shoot date was just a few weeks away. So, we pivoted. Rather than hire an experienced actor, we would instead rely on our two unproven brand ambassadors to costar in the campaign.

As the shoot date approached, I became more and more skeptical of the concept. We needed to back out. Except we couldn't. Citing the potential of upsetting our agency partner, my boss directed me to keep moving forward. So I did.

The content was shot, the fill-ins did an admirable job under the circumstances, and the video launched to icy reviews (internally and externally). To this day, it's the one project from my career that I look back on with regret. It should have never happened. It was my job as gatekeeper of the brand to **know when to walk away**. Hard to do or not, I should have broken up with the project when I had the chance.

"IT IS IMPOSSIBLE TO LIVE WITHOUT

FAILING

AT SOMETHING, UNLESS YOU LIVE

SO CAUTIOUSLY

THAT YOU MIGHT AS WELL

NOT HAVE LIVED

AT ALL."

—J. K. ROWLING

HOMEWORK

Describe a time in which your marketing efforts failed.

What were the consequences?

If you could go back in time, would you pull the plug rather than going through with it? Why? Why not?

Is there a campaign or project you are currently working on that should not move forward? Describe why.

EVERY-ONE'S PRODUCT SUCKS AT SOME POINT

RULE #14

Your product sucks. Or at least it will. Eventually you're going to come out with a concept that doesn't work the way you had hoped. When that time comes, don't force it. Rather than pretending everything is all right and pushing insincere marketing down your audience's throat for the sake of a sales forecast, pull the plug. Admit defeat and move on. If you don't, if you choose to instead get behind what you (and your consumers) know to be a flawed invention, you will lose the community's trust. And in some cases, that faith in your brand won't come back. Word will spread from one consumer to another until your next product, which truly is extraordinary, fails to reach expectations. Those short-term sales gains you enjoyed by backing a farce will quickly erode into long-term losses and consumer skepticism, all because you were too stubborn to accept reality.

Everyone's product sucks at some point. The trick is having the confidence to admit it.

31%

ACCORDING TO THE *LOS ANGELES TIMES*, MORE PEOPLE ARE AFRAID OF FAILURE (31%) THAN SPIDERS (30%), GHOSTS (15%), AND BEING HOME ALONE (9%).

HOMEWORK

Describe a time when you felt betrayed or deceived by a brand, a product, or a person.

Describe your relationship with that brand, product, or person prior to this incident.

Describe your relationship with that brand, product, or person since this incident.

How has your relationship changed?

"ZITS ARE BEAUTY MARKS."

—KURT COBAIN

STOP LYING

RULE #15

If it's not true to your brand, don't say it, don't post it, don't pretend to be it. Strong brands are built on a foundation of authenticity. There is no acting for the sake of others. There is only passion and pride in the company's mission. The moment you construct a false narrative is the moment you become vulnerable. In an era of digital truth hunters, the facts will emerge. Your brand's deceits will surface, and when they do, you'll lose all credibility. Not only will your consumers suddenly question your intentions and their own purchasing decisions, but the media will put you squarely in the crosshairs. They'll wait for the next opportunity to fire a brand-crippling headline your way.

Scared yet? You should be. But there's an easy way to avoid such a terminal fate.

Stop lying.

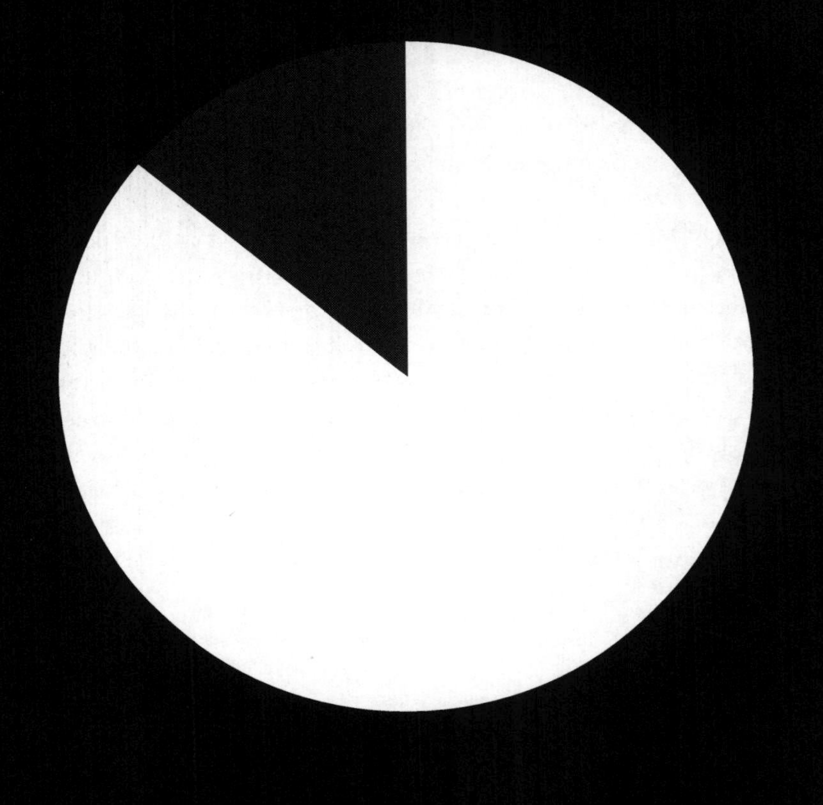

86%

ACCORDING TO A 2017 SURVEY DONE BY SOCIAL MEDIA TODAY, "86% OF PEOPLE SAY AUTHENTICITY IS IMPORTANT WHEN DECIDING WHAT BRANDS THEY LIKE AND SUPPORT."

HOMEWORK

DATE ....

Describe your brand's personality using single words or short phrases. (See pages 134 and 135 for a list of adjectives.)

....
....
....
....
....
....
....
....
....
....
....
....
....
....
....
....
....
....

Now ask a group of nonemployees to put a check mark next to the one, two, or three words or phrases from your list that they most associate with your brand.

Rank the most popular choices in order.

The most common selections reveal the crossover between what you believe your brand to be and what your consumer perceives it to be.

HOMEWORK+12

Twelve months after you've completed your initial homework assignment on the preceding pages, come back to this rule and fill out the below to reflect your brand's current state.

DATE ....

Describe your brand's personality using single words or short phrases:

....

....

....

....

....

....

....

....

....

....

....

....

....

....

....

Now ask a group of nonemployees to put a check mark next to the three words or phrases from your list that they most associate with your brand.

Rank the most popular choices in order.

HOMEWORK

If you're struggling to describe your brand, use this list of adjectives to help get you started.

Circle the words that you believe best describe your brand's personality.

Narrow down your list to ten words and write them in the corresponding space on the previously completed homework assignment.

Abrasive
Active
Adaptable
Adventuresome
Adventurous
Ambitious
Appreciative
Authentic
Balanced
Bold
Brave
Bubbly
Capable
Carefree
Caring
Cheerful
Compassionate
Concerned
Confident
Conscientious
Considerate
Courageous
Creative
Curious
Daring
Dedicated
Dependable
Determined
Devoted
Diligent
Direct
Directed
Discriminating
Distinct
Dynamic
Eager
Easygoing
Empathetic
Enduring
Energetic
Enthusiastic
Ethical
Exceptional
Excited
Exuberant
Fair
Fascinating
Feisty
Flexible
Forgiving
Friendly
Fun
Generous
Gentle
Genuine
Giving
Hardworking
Healthy
Helpful
Honest

Honorable
Humble
Humorous
Imaginative
Independent
Ingenious
Inquisitive
Insightful
Integrity
Intelligent
Interesting
Jolly
Jovial
Joyful
Keen
Kind
Knowledgeable
Laid-back
Lighthearted
Likable
Lively
Loveable
Loving
Loyal
Magical
Mannerly
Measured
Memorable
Modest
Motivated
Natural
Neat
Noble
Nurturing
Open-minded
Optimistic
Organized
Original
Outgoing
Patient
Patriotic
Peaceful
Perky
Persevering
Persistent
Pleasant
Popular
Positive
Principled
Problem solver
Proud
Quick-witted
Quiet
Rational
Real
Reasonable
Reflective
Resilient
Resourceful
Respectful
Responsible
Self-confident
Self-directed
Self-sacrificing
Self-starter
Sensitive
Sharp
Sincere
Skillful
Smart
Sociable
Spirited
Spiritual
Stable
Steady
Strong
Studious
Successful
Supportive
Surprising
Sympathetic
Thorough
Thoughtful
Tireless
Tolerant
Trusting
Trustworthy
Truthful
Unbridled
Unselfish
Upbeat
Vigilant
Warm
Wise
Witty
Wonderful
Wry

“IF YOU DON’T BELIEVE THE

SINGER,

YOU WON’T BELIEVE THE

SONG.”

—TOM PETTY

WHAT MAKES YOU DIFFERENT IS WHAT MAKES YOU A BRAND

RULE #16

Whether you're building a personal brand or starting a new business, differentiation is the key to breaking through the noise. And there's a lot of noise today. With over seven billion people on earth and twenty-eight million small businesses in the US alone, it's more difficult than ever for brands to stand out. Difficult, but not impossible.

In my early twenties, I took that initial step. While sitting in (and zoning out of) a meeting at my first corporate job, I realized I wanted to work for myself one day. I also recognized I wasn't alone. I needed to distinguish myself. **What makes you different is what makes you a brand.**

I homed in on marketing, but predictably my target wasn't distinct enough. Sports marketing? Better, but still crowded. Brand marketing in sports? Closer, but I wasn't alone yet. Brand marketing in *college* sports? Bingo. I had found my vacant plot of land; now I just needed to start building on it.

It began with writing my first book, *Brands Win Championships*, the only book dedicated to developing college sports brands. Different. I followed that up by running brand marketing for Adidas football and baseball (including the college varieties of each). Different. From there I launched a sports marketing think tank (Brand Food), wrote my second book (*Athletes Are Brands Too*), and started my own consultancy (DARLOW). Different, different, and different. Every step I took, I took in an effort to distinguish my brand. It worked.

Today, I have the great fortune of spending my days writing in coffee shops and working in an industry I love. It's a dream made possible by the power of differentiation.

If I can stand out, you can too.

MY JOURNEY TO FIND A UNIQUE SLICE OF THE MARKETING PIE:

1. MARKETING

THERE ARE FAR TOO MANY MARKETERS IN THE WORLD TO BREAK THROUGH WITHOUT FIRST CARVING OUT A NICHE.

2. MARKETING IN SPORTS

WHILE SPORTS MARKETING IS A SMALLER COMMUNITY TO CONTEND WITH, THERE REMAINED PLENTY OF SPORTS TEAMS AND ATHLETES SUPPORTED BY MARKETERS; I NEEDED MORE FOCUS.

3. BRAND MARKETING IN SPORTS

ADDING "BRAND" TO THE EQUATION ELIMINATED MUCH OF THE COMPETITION; HOWEVER, I WASN'T ALONE, AND THAT WAS (AND IS) THE GOAL.

4. BRAND MARKETING IN COLLEGE SPORTS

I FOUND MY NICHE. THERE WERE NO EXPERTS SPEAKING ON WAYS TO USE BRAND MARKETING IN COLLEGE SPORTS. I WAS ALONE AND READY TO CARVE OUT MY OWN SLICE OF THE MARKETING PIE.

HOMEWORK

List the words and phrases the competition is using to describe their brand.

COMPETITOR ....
DESCRIPTION ....
DESCRIPTION ....
DESCRIPTION ....
DESCRIPTION ....

COMPETITOR ....
DESCRIPTION ....
DESCRIPTION ....
DESCRIPTION ....
DESCRIPTION ....

COMPETITOR ....
DESCRIPTION ....
DESCRIPTION ....
DESCRIPTION ....
DESCRIPTION ....

COMPETITOR ....
DESCRIPTION ....
DESCRIPTION ....
DESCRIPTION ....
DESCRIPTION ....

COMPETITOR ....
DESCRIPTION ....
DESCRIPTION ....
DESCRIPTION ....
DESCRIPTION ....

COMPETITOR ....
DESCRIPTION ....
DESCRIPTION ....
DESCRIPTION ....
DESCRIPTION ....

List the words and phrases your brand is using to describe itself.

YOUR BRAND ....
DESCRIPTION ....
DESCRIPTION ....
DESCRIPTION ....
DESCRIPTION ....
DESCRIPTION ....
DESCRIPTION ....
DESCRIPTION ....
DESCRIPTION ....
DESCRIPTION ....

Now cross out any words or phrases that you listed under your brand that can also be found listed under a competitor's name. The words or phrases that remain on your brand's list of descriptors are potential areas of brand differentiation.

"THE THINGS THAT MAKE US DIFFERENT, THOSE ARE OUR SUPER-POWERS."

—LENA WAITHE

HOMEWORK

What are the general stereotypes associated with brands in your industry?

STEREOTYPE ....

STEREOTYPE ....

STEREOTYPE ....

STEREOTYPE ....

STEREOTYPE ....

STEREOTYPE ....

STEREOTYPE ....

STEREOTYPE ....

STEREOTYPE ....

STEREOTYPE ....

STEREOTYPE ....

STEREOTYPE ....

STEREOTYPE ....

STEREOTYPE ....

STEREOTYPE ....

STEREOTYPE ....

STEREOTYPE ....

STEREOTYPE ....

STEREOTYPE ....

STEREOTYPE ....

STEREOTYPE ....

STEREOTYPE ....

STEREOTYPE ....

STEREOTYPE ....

Does your brand disprove any of these stereotypes? If so, which and how?

STEREOTYPE ....
HOW? ....

STEREOTYPE ....
HOW? ....

STEREOTYPE ....
HOW? ....

STEREOTYPE ....
HOW? ....

STEREOTYPE ....
HOW? ....

STEREOTYPE ....
HOW? ....

STEREOTYPE ....
HOW? ....

STEREOTYPE ....
HOW? ....

STEREOTYPE ....
HOW? ....

(NON-DIFFERENTIATED) BRAND

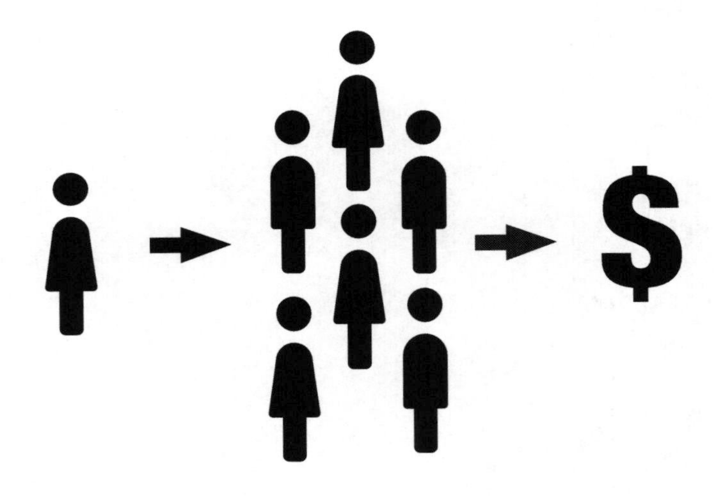

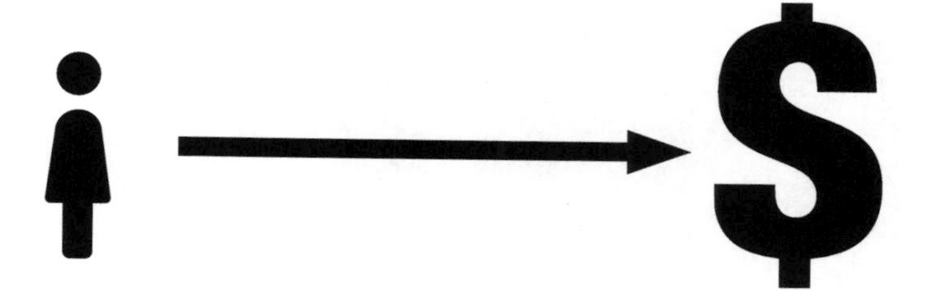

BRAND **COMPETITION** **MARKET SHARE**

The less differentiated your brand is, the more competitors there are standing between you and the market share you need to succeed. As Mark Cuban is often credited for saying, "When you've got 10,000 people trying to do the same thing, why would you want to be 10,001?"

BE
THE
ONLY

RULE #17

There is no more powerful word in brand marketing than the word *only*, as in the only brand to provide a specific product or service. In my experience, either you're standing out, or you're blending in. There is no gray area. A company's ability to claim exclusive ownership of a defined slice of the industry pie is the purest form of brand differentiation and the quickest way to avoid falling victim to industry homogeny. Your goal, as you set out to establish your own brand position (see DARLOW Rule #18), should be to identify a market space like this in which you, and you alone, reside. **Be the only.**

One of my favorite executions of this rule is Apple's iMac computer, released in 1998 as the only desktop workstation of the time to come in a variety of colors. In a world filled with dreary, beige boxes, the iMac stood out thanks to its grape-, lime-, strawberry-, and tangerine-tinted monitors. And while the computer itself was hailed by the company to be as functional as the competition, if not more so, the true differentiator came in how it looked.

Apple may not have had the *only* internet-ready computer in the market at the time, but they did have the *only* internet-ready computer available in a variety of fruity colors.

That's different.

ARE YOU AN "X"?

OR THE “O”?

HOMEWORK

List the types of products or services your competitors provide.

COMPETITOR ....
PRODUCT/SERVICE ....
PRODUCT/SERVICE ....
PRODUCT/SERVICE ....
PRODUCT/SERVICE ....

COMPETITOR ....
PRODUCT/SERVICE ....
PRODUCT/SERVICE ....
PRODUCT/SERVICE ....
PRODUCT/SERVICE ....

COMPETITOR ....
PRODUCT/SERVICE ....
PRODUCT/SERVICE ....
PRODUCT/SERVICE ....
PRODUCT/SERVICE ....

COMPETITOR ....
PRODUCT/SERVICE ....
PRODUCT/SERVICE ....
PRODUCT/SERVICE ....
PRODUCT/SERVICE ....

List the types of products or services your brand provides.

YOUR BRAND ....

PRODUCT/SERVICE ....

PRODUCT/SERVICE ....

PRODUCT/SERVICE ....

PRODUCT/SERVICE ....

PRODUCT/SERVICE ....

PRODUCT/SERVICE ....

PRODUCT/SERVICE ....

PRODUCT/SERVICE ....

PRODUCT/SERVICE ....

PRODUCT/SERVICE ....

PRODUCT/SERVICE ....

PRODUCT/SERVICE ....

PRODUCT/SERVICE ....

PRODUCT/SERVICE ....

PRODUCT/SERVICE ....

PRODUCT/SERVICE ....

PRODUCT/SERVICE ....

PRODUCT/SERVICE ....

PRODUCT/SERVICE ....

PRODUCT/SERVICE ....

PRODUCT/SERVICE ....

PRODUCT/SERVICE ....

PRODUCT/SERVICE ....

Now cross out any products or services that you listed under your brand that can also be found listed under a competitor's name. The products or services remaining on your brand's list are potential areas of differentiation.

HOMEWORK

What are the physical features of your brand or product that stand out from the competition?

PHYSICAL FEATURE ....
PHYSICAL FEATURE ....
PHYSICAL FEATURE ....
PHYSICAL FEATURE ....
PHYSICAL FEATURE ....
PHYSICAL FEATURE ....
PHYSICAL FEATURE ....
PHYSICAL FEATURE ....
PHYSICAL FEATURE ....
PHYSICAL FEATURE ....
PHYSICAL FEATURE ....
PHYSICAL FEATURE ....
PHYSICAL FEATURE ....
PHYSICAL FEATURE ....
PHYSICAL FEATURE ....
PHYSICAL FEATURE ....
PHYSICAL FEATURE ....
PHYSICAL FEATURE ....
PHYSICAL FEATURE ....
PHYSICAL FEATURE ....
PHYSICAL FEATURE ....
PHYSICAL FEATURE ....

What physical features can be developed or added to your brand or product in order to differentiate it?

PHYSICAL FEATURE ....
PHYSICAL FEATURE ....
PHYSICAL FEATURE ....
PHYSICAL FEATURE ....
PHYSICAL FEATURE ....
PHYSICAL FEATURE ....
PHYSICAL FEATURE ....
PHYSICAL FEATURE ....
PHYSICAL FEATURE ....
PHYSICAL FEATURE ....
PHYSICAL FEATURE ....
PHYSICAL FEATURE ....
PHYSICAL FEATURE ....
PHYSICAL FEATURE ....
PHYSICAL FEATURE ....
PHYSICAL FEATURE ....
PHYSICAL FEATURE ....
PHYSICAL FEATURE ....
PHYSICAL FEATURE ....
PHYSICAL FEATURE ....
PHYSICAL FEATURE ....
PHYSICAL FEATURE ....
PHYSICAL FEATURE ....
PHYSICAL FEATURE ....

THE DARLOW DIFFERENTIATION METHOD

Once you finish analyzing your brand, the industry, and your competition, use the DARLOW Differentiation Method to determine the areas in which your brand is both unique and powerful.

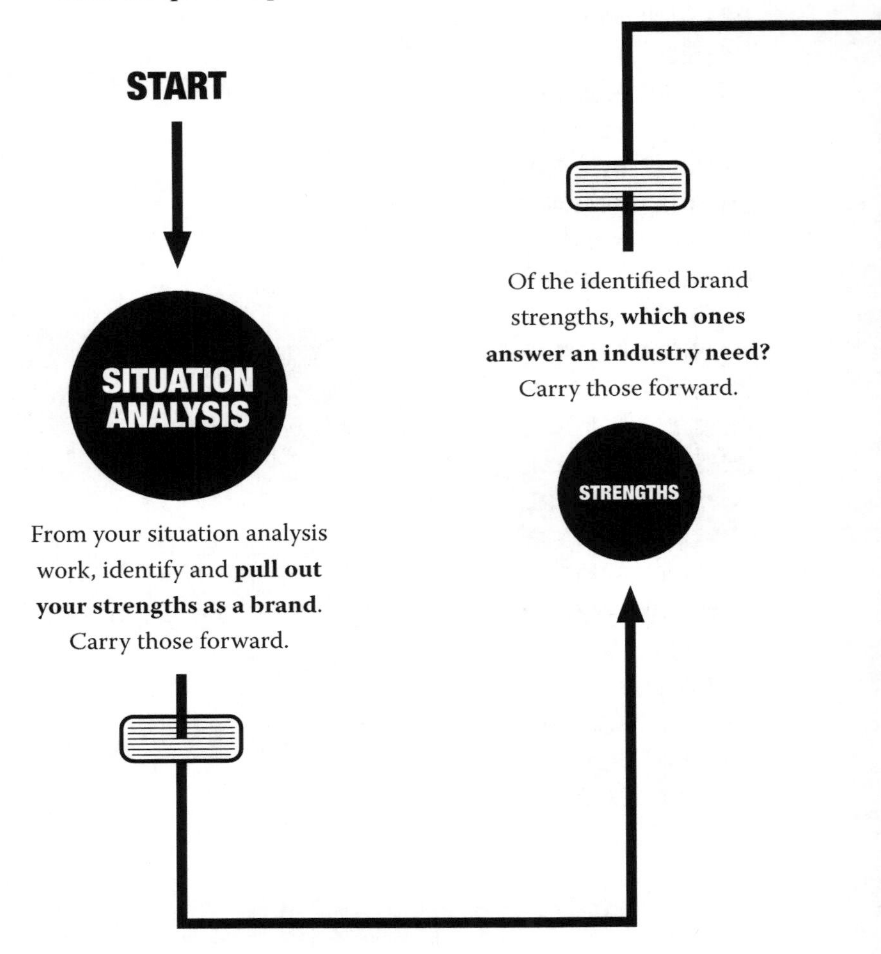

START
SITUATION ANALYSIS
From your situation analysis work, identify and **pull out your strengths as a brand**. Carry those forward.
STRENGTHS
Of the identified brand strengths, **which ones answer an industry need?** Carry those forward.

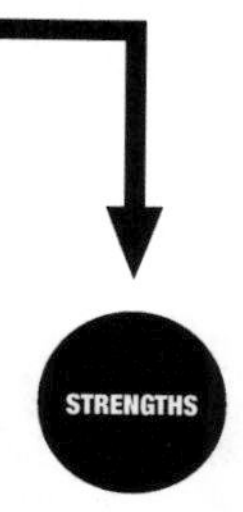

Of the remaining brand strengths, **which ones are differentiated from your competition?**
Carry those forward.

FINISH

What you are left with are **areas in which your brand is:**

1. **Strong**
2. **Relevant**
3. **Differentiated**

Consider choosing one of these remaining areas when determining your point of difference in the homework for Rule #18.

NO
POSITIONING,
NO
DIFFERENTIATION,
NO
BRAND

RULE #18

We've reached the most important element of your marketing plan: the brand positioning statement. This, by my own definition, is the single sentence, used internally, that describes what makes your brand unique among the competition. Given today's embarrassment of options, why are consumers going to choose you over your rivals? Your sentence should clearly and concisely answer that question. If not, you're just blending in. **No positioning, no differentiation, no brand.** Now, if that sounds unnerving, don't worry. I'll walk you through the process. In the homework section of this rule, you will take the steps necessary to build your own statement.

When you complete this rule and finalize your brand's positioning statement, treat the result as your north star, keeping you on track through good times and bad. Once established, all campaigns must be developed with the explicit purpose of building equity in and ownership of your position. Before you sign off on that television commercial, that late-night tweet, or that new product launch, make sure it feeds your big-picture positioning strategy. Anything else is (gulp) "off brand" and a waste of your time.

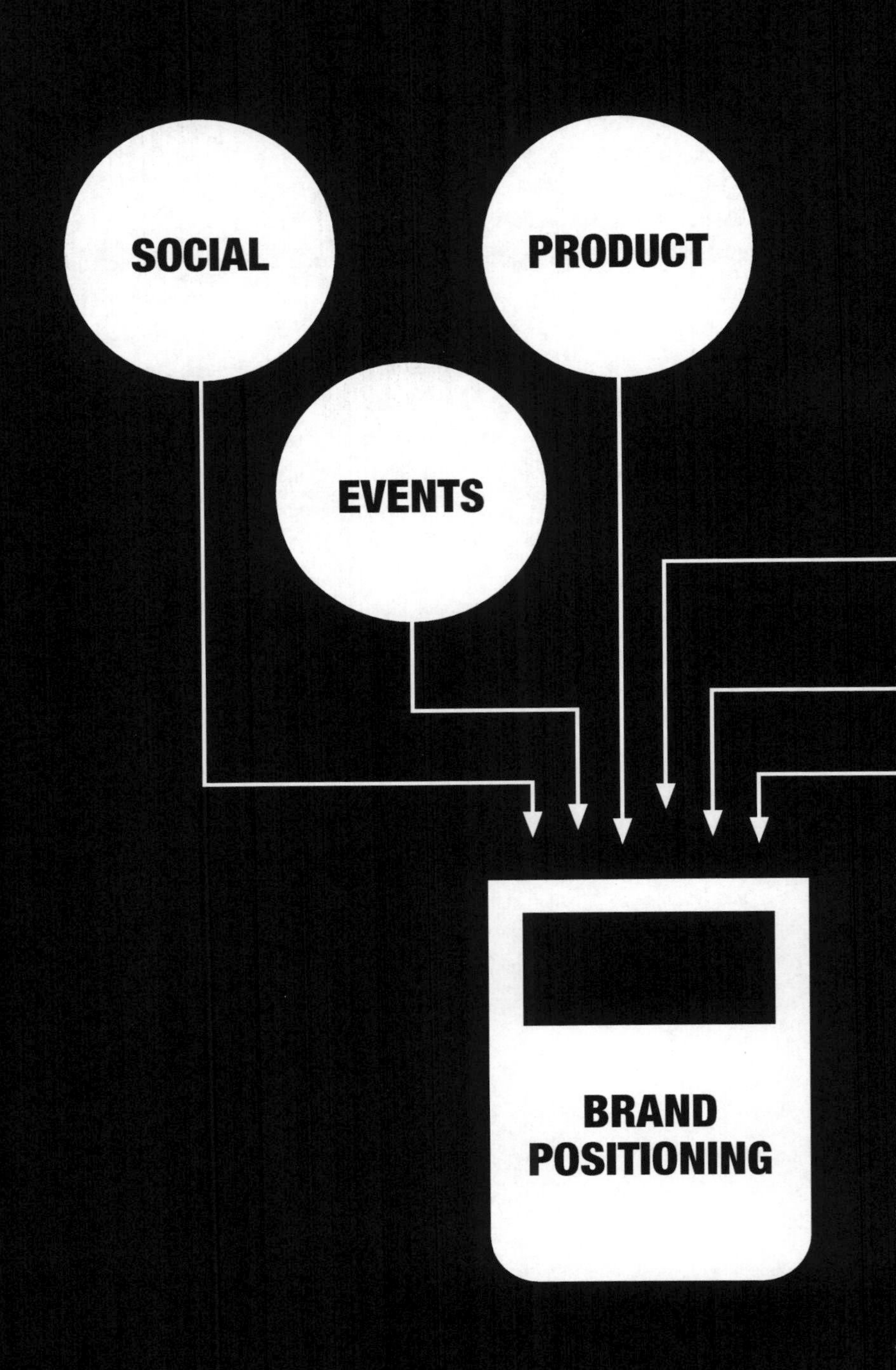
SOCIAL
PRODUCT
EVENTS
BRAND
POSITIONING

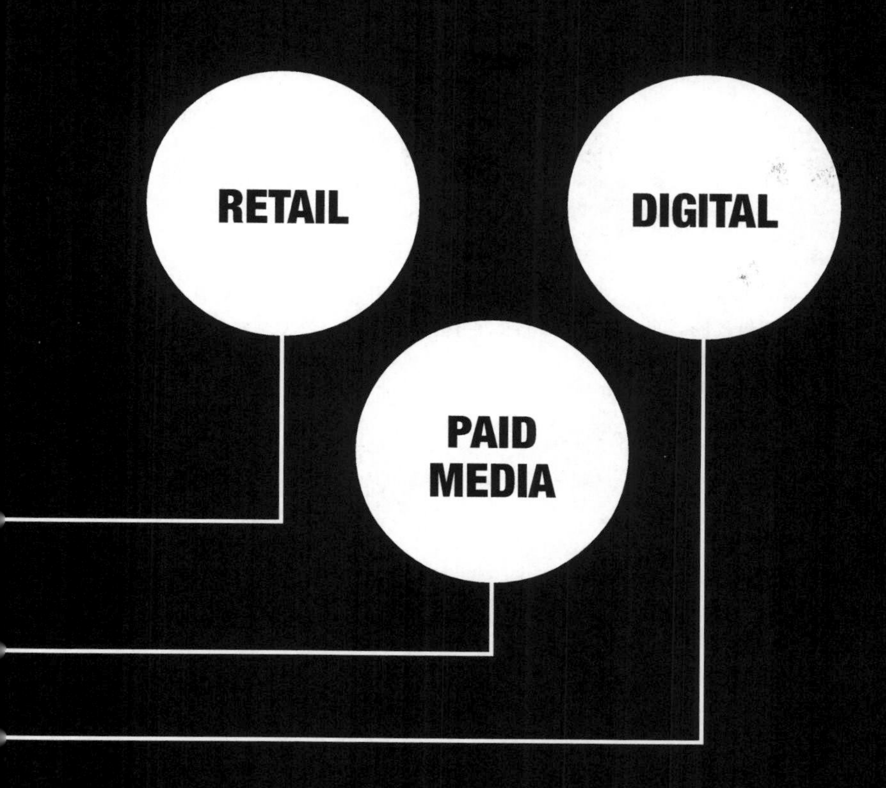

EVERYTHING YOU DO AS A COMPANY SHOULD BE DONE WITH THE EXPLICIT PURPOSE OF BUILDING EQUITY IN AND OWNERSHIP OF YOUR BRAND'S POSITION.

HOMEWORK

Now that you've identified what it is that makes your brand unique among your competition, define your positioning statement by completing the following three steps.

STEP ONE

IDENTIFY YOUR FRAME OF REFERENCE: A frame of reference is the space in which you are competing. In my case, "marketing executives" is my frame of reference, as in the community or industry in which I need to differentiate myself as a brand. This phrase will make up the first half of your final positioning statement.

DARLOW IS THE MARKETING EXECUTIVE . . .

Now fill in your own frame of reference:
(insert brand name) is the (insert frame of reference) . . .

....

STEP TWO

DEFINE YOUR POINT OF DIFFERENCE: The point of difference is what makes your brand unique within your frame of reference. For me, focusing on "helping college athletes, coaches, and teams build their brands" is what makes my personal brand distinct as compared to other marketing executives. This phrase will make up the second half of your final positioning statement.

. . . HELPING COLLEGE ATHLETES, COACHES, AND TEAMS BUILD THEIR BRANDS

Now fill in your own point of difference:

....

STEP THREE

FINALIZE YOUR POSITIONING STATEMENT: Now combine your frame of reference and point of difference to create a single positioning statement.

DARLOW IS THE MARKETING EXECUTIVE HELPING COLLEGE ATHLETES, COACHES, AND TEAMS BUILD THEIR BRANDS.

Now complete your positioning statement:

....

....

Note that your positioning statement is not a tagline or intended to be clever. Be as literal and to the point as possible. Your sentence is not going on a billboard or in a magazine; it's simply a guidepost meant to keep you and your employees on track while directing the brand's voice and actions moving forward.

HOMEWORK

If you forget or are still unclear on what a positioning statement is, just take a look at your hand. Believe it or not, each of our fingers has its own differentiated brand. In this case, the frame of reference in which each competes is other fingers. For instance, the thumb's challenge is to differentiate itself from its four finger rivals: index, middle, ring, and pinky.

To demonstrate how each has its own unique brand, draw a line from the five points of difference listed here to the appropriate finger brand.

1. Equipped to wear a wedding ring
2. Designed to make unbreakable promises
3. Most often used by hitchhikers
4. Pointing you in the right direction
5. Best at expressing anger toward another

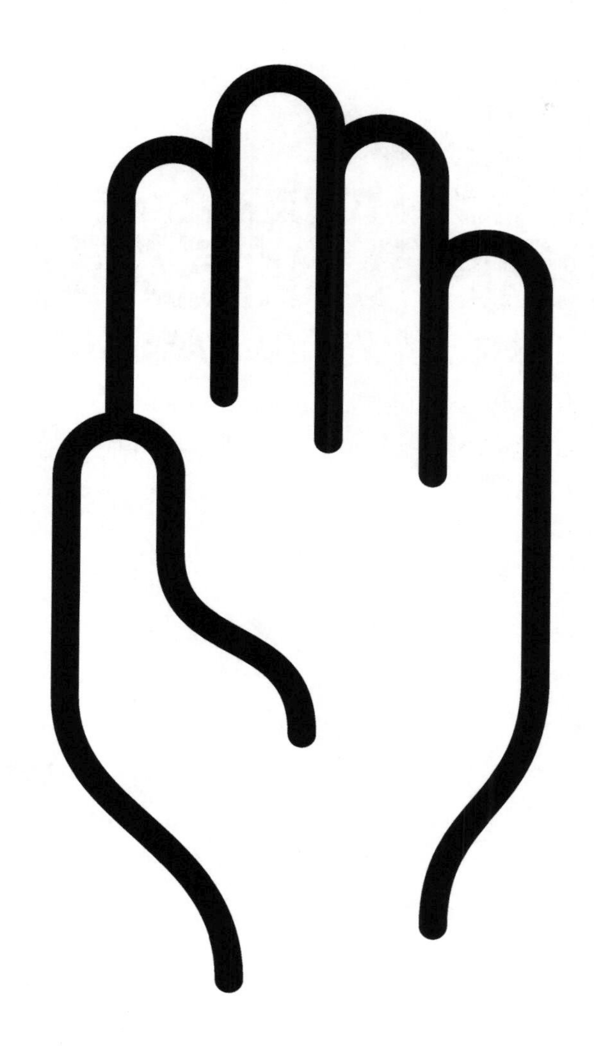

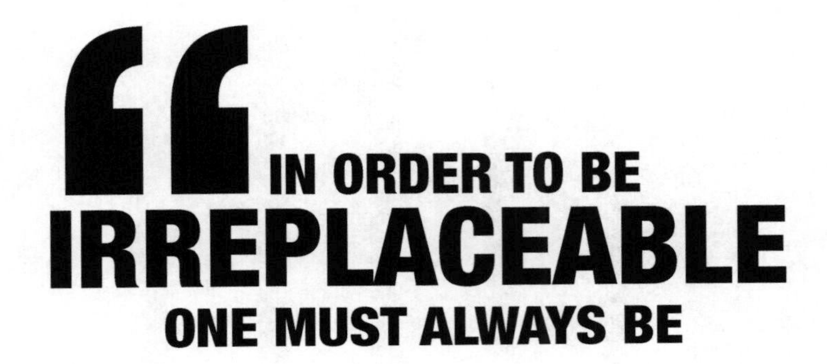

"IN ORDER TO BE
IRREPLACEABLE
ONE MUST ALWAYS BE

DIFFERENT."

—COCO CHANEL

IF YOU CAN'T SEE IT, YOU CAN'T AFFECT IT

RULE #19

The patch of overgrown weeds surrounding you is not only obscuring your vision, it's killing your brand. And it's your fault. Search rankings have suffered, traffic to your site is on the decline, and your events look more like ghost towns than they do parties. But you can't see any of that; all you can see is tomorrow's Instagram story. You're lost in the social media weeds, and your brand is failing because of it. The problem? Your point of view.

A brand director who spends more time executing (from the ground) than supervising (from the sky) is doing more harm than good. That's not the job. Brand management is not about writing tweets and taking pretty pictures; it's about observation. Your job is to keep tabs on everything related to the person, product, or service you're responsible for, ensuring that all parts of the machine continue to feed a single positioning strategy. That's an impossible task when all you can see is one part of that machine.

Step back. Way back. In fact, manage your brand like an airline pilot sees the world, from thirty thousand feet. At any point in the day, you need to be able to comprehend and identify what's working and not working in your advertising, events, paid media, and social media departments, just to name a few. **If you can't see it, you can't affect it.**

And right now, you can't see it.

VIEW FROM THE GROUND:

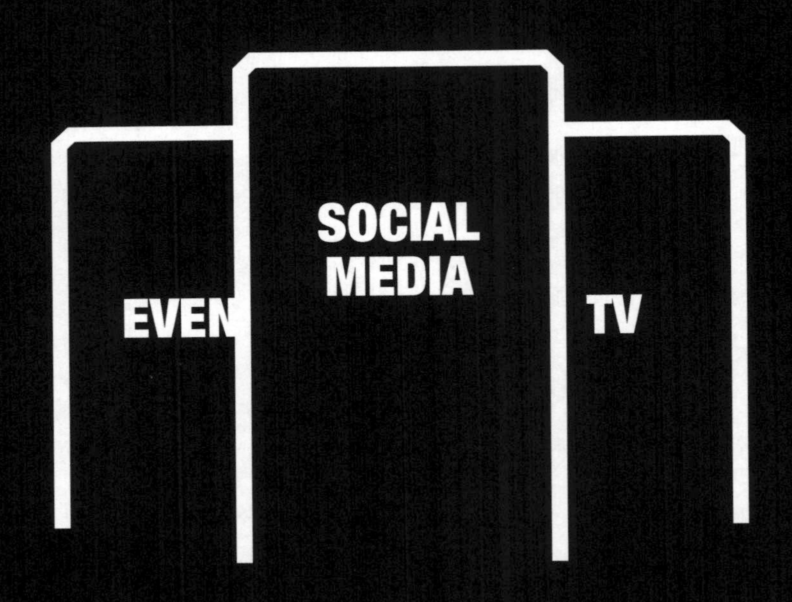

VIEW FROM THE SKY:

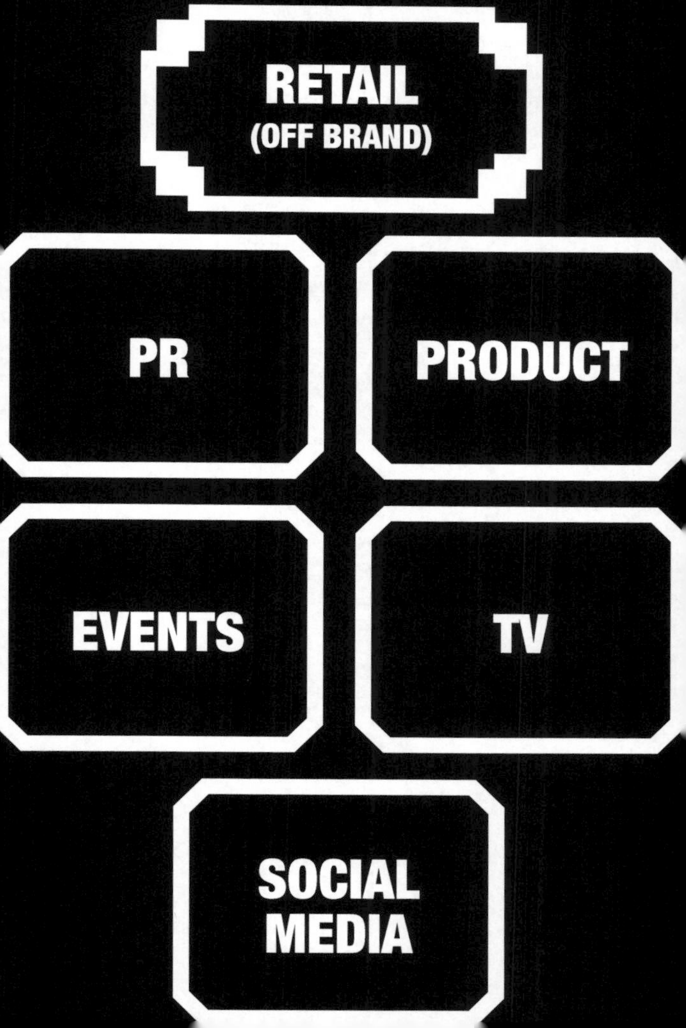

RETAIL
(OFF BRAND)

PR

PRODUCT

EVENTS

TV

SOCIAL
MEDIA

HOMEWORK

DATE ....

1. Write your positioning statement in the middle circle.

2. In the outer circles, fill in the current communication platforms you use to promote your brand (Twitter, Instagram, television, radio, etc.).

3. Without looking it up, on the line connecting the platform to your positioning statement, write out the latest brand message coming from that platform.

4. Highlight those areas in which you are unable to recall the message.

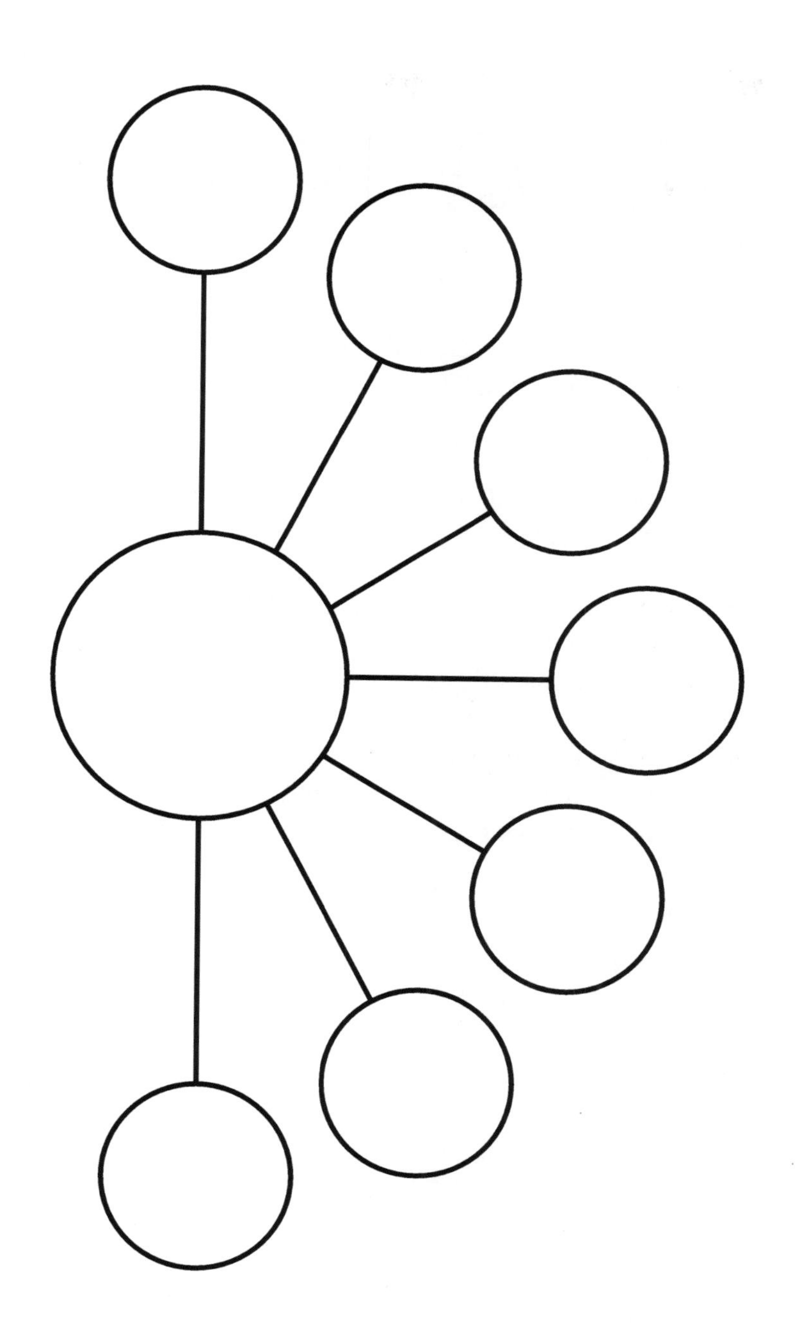

HOMEWORK+3

Three months after you've completed your initial homework assignment on the preceding pages, come back to this rule and fill out the following page to reflect your brand's current state.

DATE ....

1. Write your positioning statement in the middle circle.

2. In the outer circles, fill in the current communication platforms you use to promote your brand (Twitter, Instagram, television, radio, etc.).

3. Without looking it up, on the line connecting the platform to your positioning statement, write out the latest brand message coming from that platform.

4. Highlight those areas in which you are unable to recall the message.

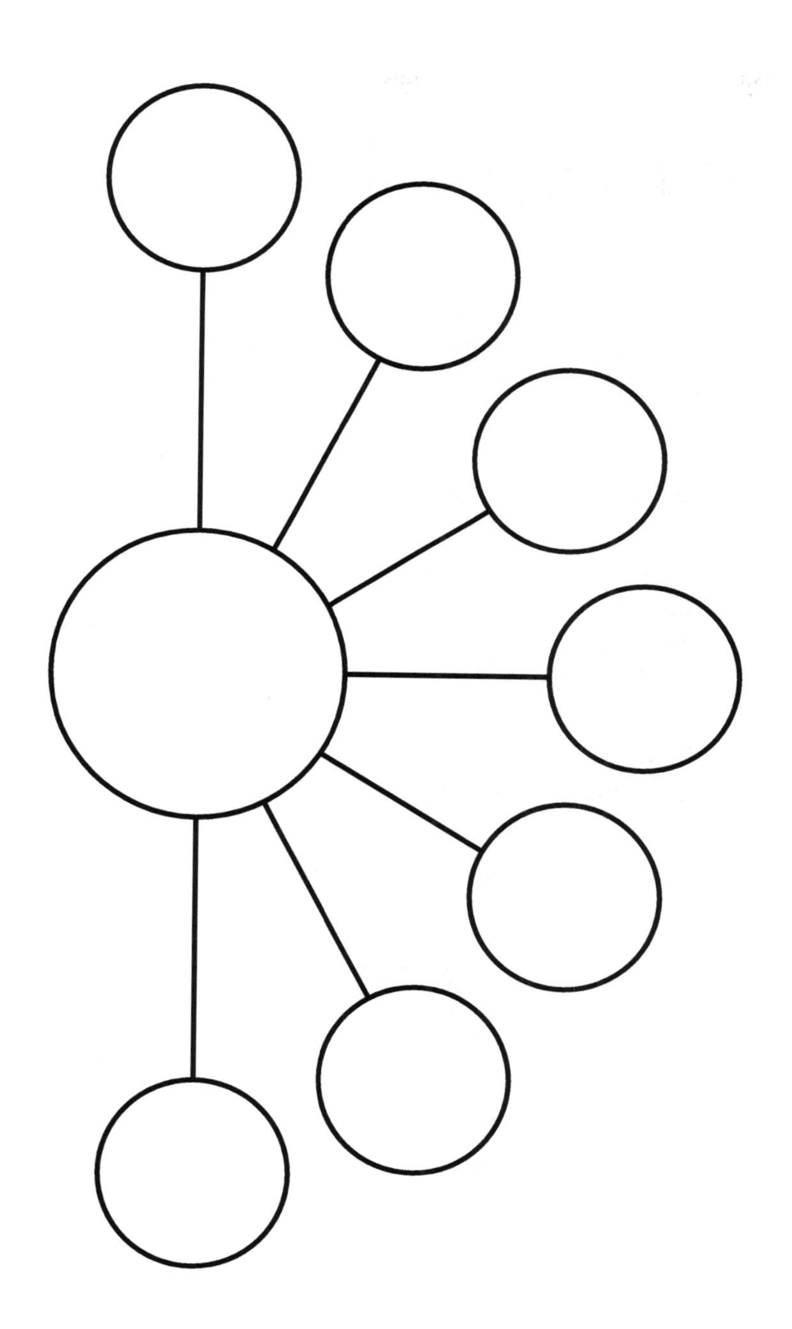

HOMEWORK+6

Six months after you've completed your HOMEWORK+3 assignment on the preceding pages, come back to this rule and fill out the following page to reflect your brand's current state.

DATE ....

1. Write your positioning statement in the middle circle.

2. In the outer circles, fill in the current communication platforms you use to promote your brand (Twitter, Instagram, television, radio, etc.).

3. Without looking it up, on the line connecting the platform to your positioning statement, write out the latest brand message coming from that platform.

4. Highlight those areas in which you are unable to recall the message.

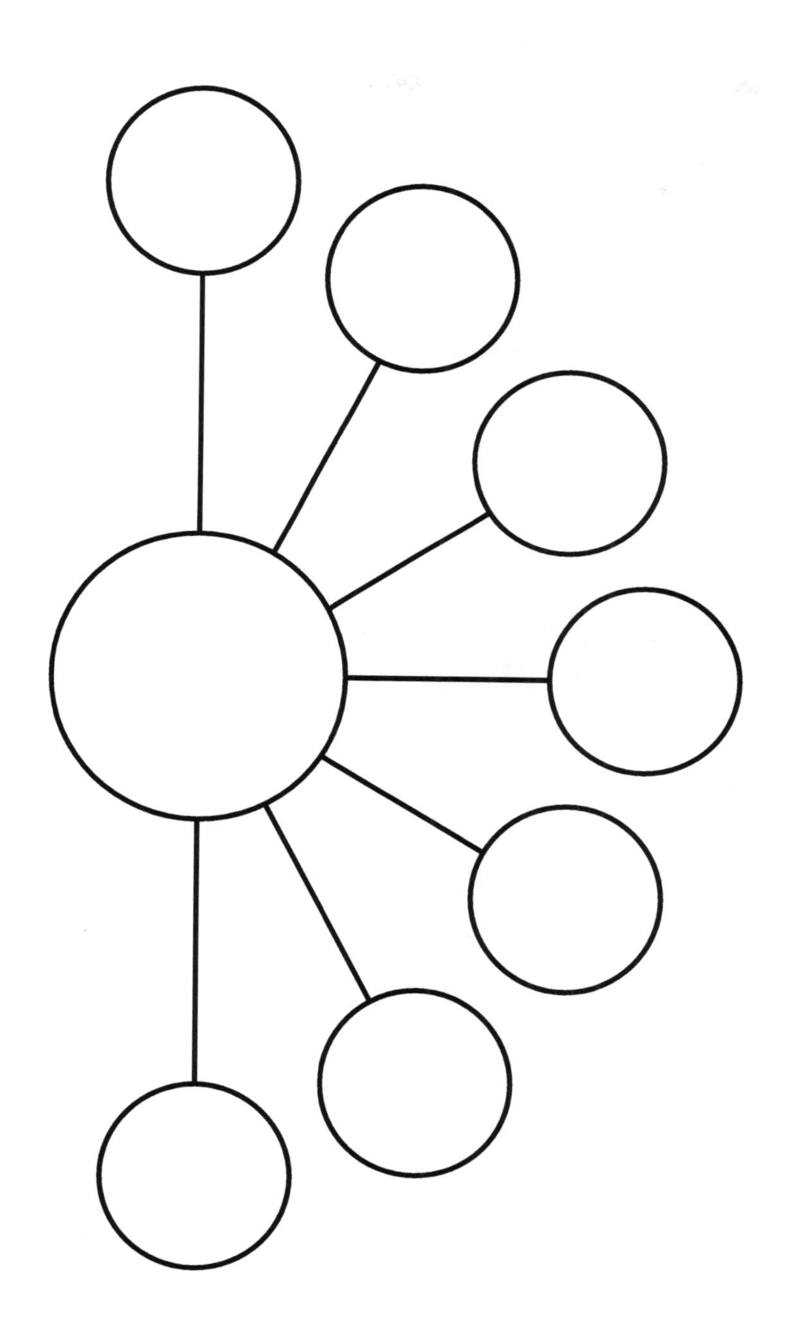

FOCUS

RULE #20

Calling someone a jack-of-all-trades is just a nice way of saying they aren't great at any one thing. When a brand gets labeled a jack-of-all-trades, it means their message is diluted and the company's position is unclear. That kind of brand ambiguity can severely hinder an organization's ability to differentiate itself among the competition. Brands are like knives: the sharper the blade, the easier it is to cut out a slice of the pie. That is, the more focused the brand, the easier it is to own a piece of the market.

Take the fast-food industry, for example. Everywhere you look, companies have made their marks by fixating on a single segment of the business. McDonald's started with hamburgers, Taco Bell with tacos, and Subway with sandwiches. In each case, because of this single-minded approach to brand segmentation, when we think of those particular food products, we also think of those brands. By concentrating on and excelling at one aspect of an industry, the brand and category eventually become synonymous.

In a world overwhelmed by choices, the dedicated thrive, while brands that attempt to be all things to all people fail to become anything to anyone. Jack and his trades are dead; long live **focus**.

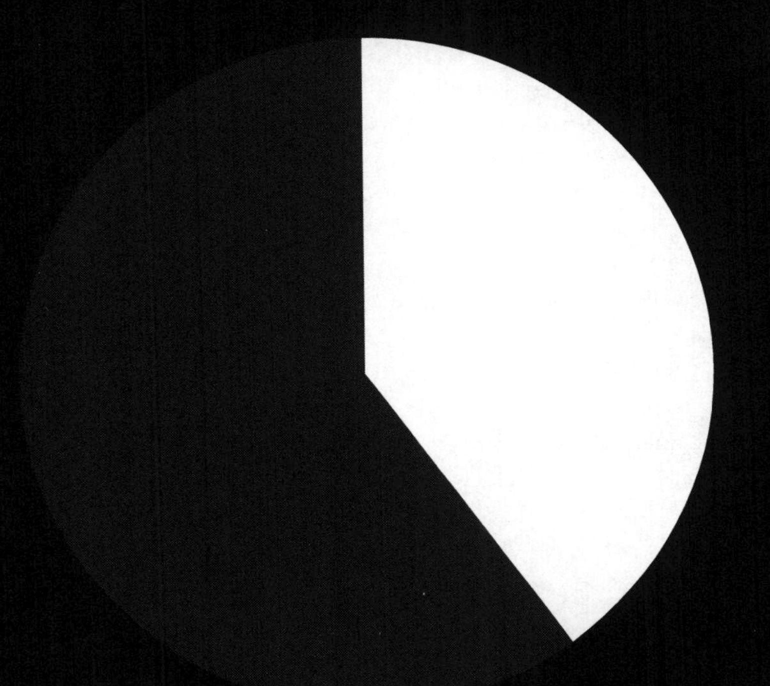

40%

ACCORDING TO MASHABLE, "FOCUSING ON MORE THAN ONE THING" DECREASES PRODUCTIVITY BY 40% AND LOWERS A PERSON'S IQ BY 10 POINTS. ADDITIONALLY, JUST 2% OF PEOPLE CAN EFFECTIVELY MULTITASK.

HOMEWORK

DATE ....

1. Write your positioning statement in the middle circle.

2. In the outer circles, fill in the current communication platforms you use to promote your brand (Twitter, Instagram, television, radio, etc.).

3. Fill in the latest brand message coming from each point of communication. While I asked you to recite this information from memory in the previous rule, you can look it up this time.

4. Highlight those areas that do not reinforce your brand's positioning statement.

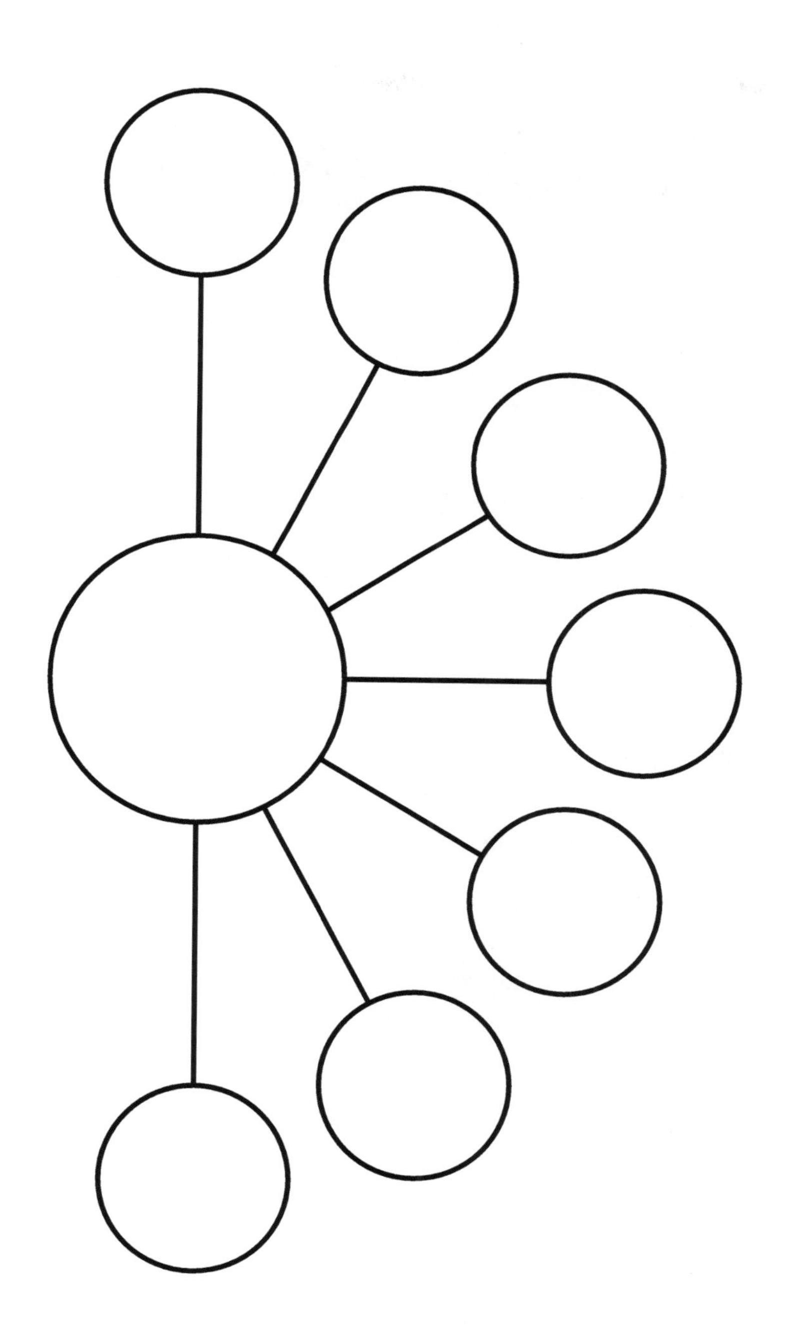

HOMEWORK+3

Three months after you've completed your initial homework assignment on the preceding pages, come back to this rule and fill out the following page to reflect your brand's current state.

DATE ....

1. Write your positioning statement in the middle circle.

2. In the outer circles, fill in the current communication platforms you use to promote your brand (Twitter, Instagram, television, radio, etc.).

3. Fill in the latest brand message coming from each point of communication. While I asked you to recite this information from memory in the previous rule, you can look it up this time.

4. Highlight those areas that do not reinforce your brand's positioning statement.

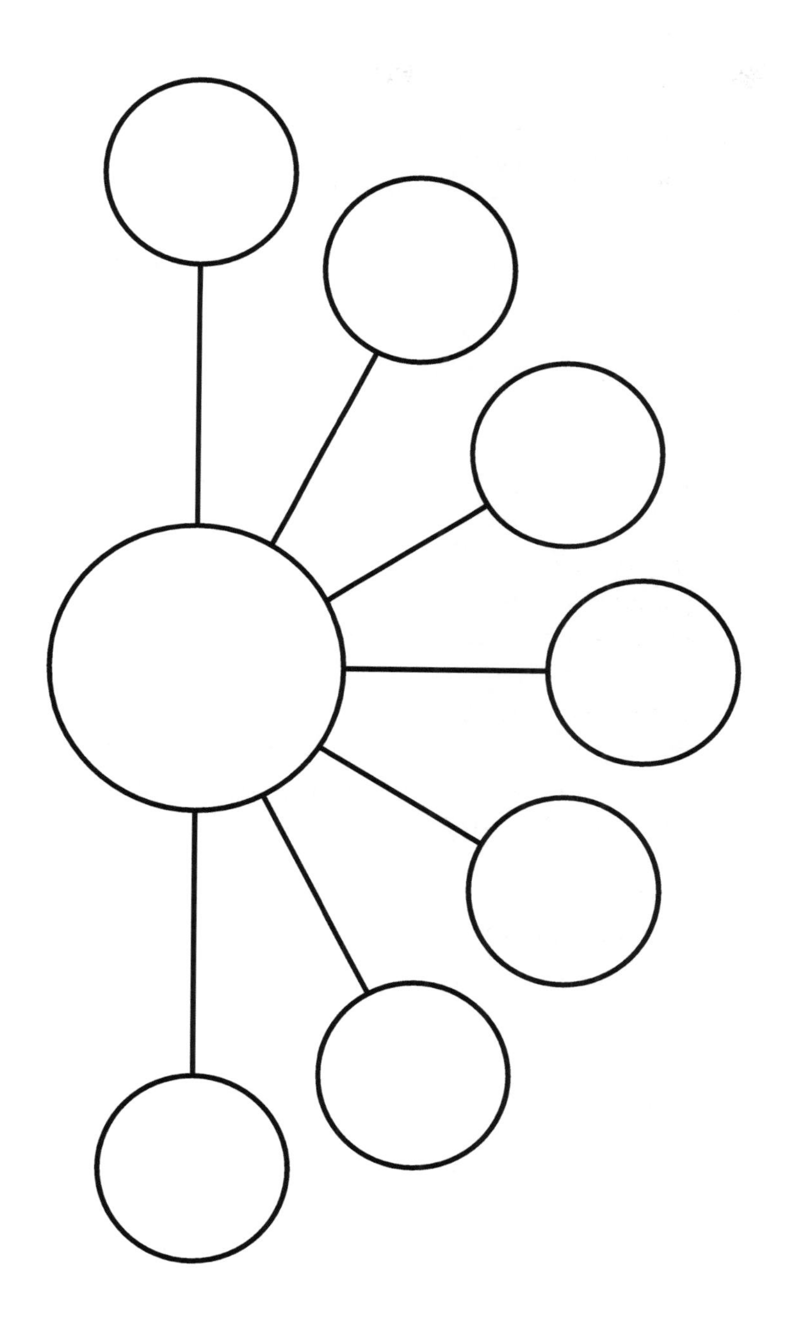

HOMEWORK+6

Six months after you've completed your HOMEWORK+3 assignment on the preceding pages, come back to this rule and fill out the following page to reflect your brand's current state.

DATE ....

1. Write your positioning statement in the middle circle.

2. In the outer circles, fill in the current communication platforms you use to promote your brand (Twitter, Instagram, television, radio, etc.).

3. Fill in the latest brand message coming from each point of communication. While I asked you to recite this information from memory in the previous rule, you can look it up this time.

4. Highlight those areas that do not reinforce your brand's positioning statement.

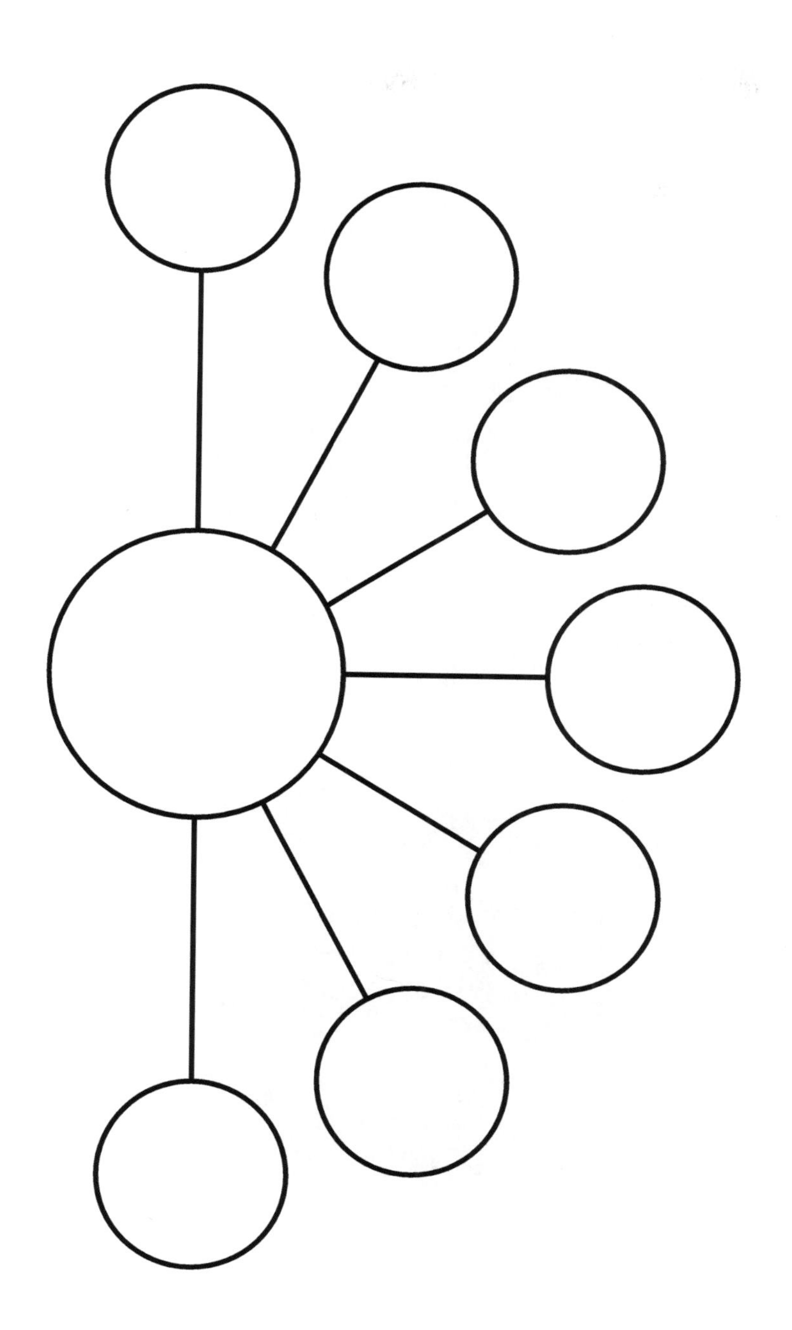

"THE SUN'S RAYS

DO NOT BURN

UNTIL BROUGHT TO A

—ALEXANDER GRAHAM BELL

PEOPLE FOLLOW LEADERS—AND LEADERS DON'T FOLLOW ANYONE

RULE #21

Those who are comfortable in their own skin are sexy. We want to be with them. Individuals who know and love themselves for who they are, are infectious. We want to be around them. Those unicorns among us who live their lives unapologetically are role models. We want to be like them. And—surprise, surprise—brands are no different.

When that upstart surf company rejects public opinion and instead carves out its own radical path, people swoon. People swoon because many strive to live their lives in a similar way but don't. It's too scary. That same public opinion, along with the responsibility, fear, and consequences that come with being an adult, gets in the way. We all have a little anarchy inside of us, but it's a brave few that actually let it out. And that's why we're attracted to the ones who do. They say what we won't, they do what we wish we could, and they refuse to worry about what other people think, including their own fans. That's why we love them. **People follow leaders—and leaders don't follow anyone.**

It's often said that humans can smell insecurity, but that's not all we can smell. Self-assurance produces an equally potent scent. The difference is one turns us off, while the other turns us on.

"NOBODY SHOULD BE ON ANYONE ELSE'S PATH."

—ELLEN DEGENERES

HOMEWORK

Make a list of people you consider comfortable in their own skin.

....
....
....
....
....
....
....
....
....
....
....

What have these individuals done to give you that impression?

....
....
....
....
....
....
....
....
....
....
....

What lessons can you take from the way these individuals carry themselves and apply to your brand?

PRODUCTS SERVE A PURPOSE; BRANDS GIVE PURPOSE

RULE #22

Products come and go, but brands can last forever. Take the iPod. The once dominant market leader in mobile music and former Apple cash cow made up approximately 40% of the company's total revenue in 2006. The same product suffered an epic fall from grace just eight years later, shrinking to 1% of the corporation's total revenue by 2014.

It's a familiar product narrative. When you're hot, you're hot. When you're not, you're not. But what's unfamiliar is the fact that, despite the demise of one of their most successful commodities, Apple as a company grew by over 800% in that same period. The brand prospered under duress. Why?

During those eight years, Apple never ceased to live by its "Think Different" mantra, introducing a range of groundbreaking technologies that included the iPhone and iPad, followed closely behind by the Apple Watch. All of these were delivered to a creative community clamoring for innovation and the social currency that came with each new release. Through it all, Apple continued to build loyalty among this group of highly influential people by leaning into an overall brand positioning strategy and company culture that proved much stronger than any single product. Today people are just as likely to buy a Mac for what the logo stands for and how it makes them feel as they are for the functionality of the computer itself. That's the hack. **Products serve a purpose; brands give purpose.**

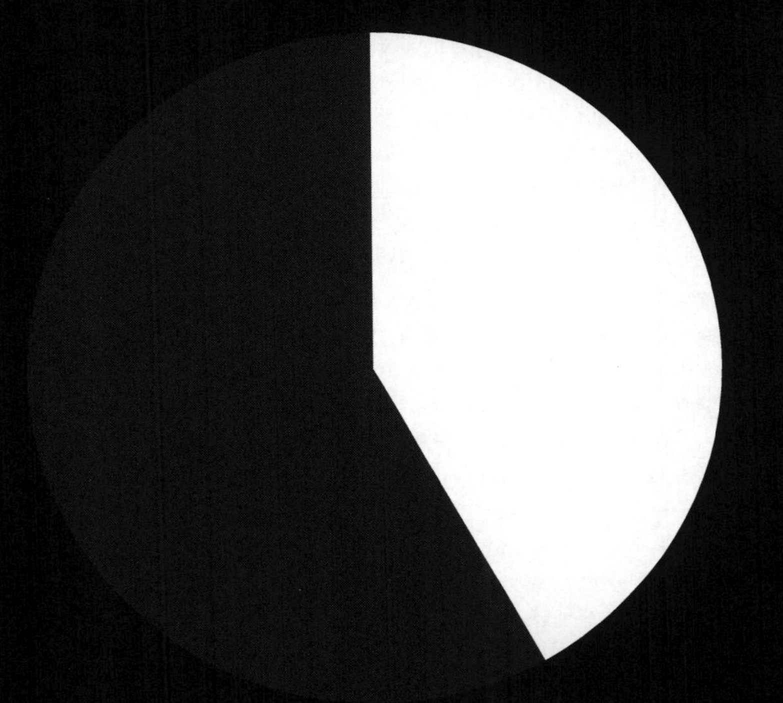

43%

ACCORDING TO FUNDERA, 43% OF CONSUMERS IN THE UNITED STATES SPEND MORE MONEY WITH BRANDS AND COMPANIES THEY ARE LOYAL TO. TRANSLATION: IT PAYS TO KEEP YOUR CONSUMERS HAPPY.

HOMEWORK

At some point your product or service will fall out of style. When that time comes, the thing that will keep your brand alive is the emotional connection you've made with your consumers. In those tumultuous times, your logo will be stronger than your product, and your fans will remain loyal because they believe in what you are, not what you sell.

Beyond the product or service you are offering, why would or why do consumers support your brand?

"IT'S MORE **FUN** TO BE A **PIRATE** THAN TO JOIN **THE NAVY.**"

—STEVE JOBS

DON'T SKIP STEPS

RULE #23

You might be surprised to learn that a brand marketer's greatest talent is patience. Not creativity or imagination. Yes, I know the "fun" part of marketing is advertising. Dreaming up the next great television campaign, writing clever Twitter copy, and doodling print ad ideas onto napkins. But until you've taken the critical step of defining your positioning statement, what it is you're building toward, your ideas are nothing more than guesses. Without that statement to guide you, you're marketing with your eyes closed. It's the brand version of pin the tail on the donkey. Sometimes you'll hit, but more often than not, you won't. Fun for you, but severely damaging to the brand. And yet the answer to avoiding such peril is simple: take a breath.

Don't let your eagerness to promote a brand take away from your ability to build one. Start from the beginning and **don't skip steps**.

“YOU CAN’T
HAVE IT ALL,
ALL AT ONCE.”

—RUTH BADER GINSBURG

HOMEWORK

Circle the previous DARLOW Rules homework assignments you have failed to complete up to this point.

1

2

3

4

5

6

7

8

9

10

11

12

13

14

15

16

17

18

19

20

21

22

Go back and finish those that you have skipped.

DON'T LISTEN TO AN IDEA UNTIL YOU HEAR AN OBJECTIVE

RULE #24

Without goals, there's no way to measure progress. And yet so many of today's marketing departments are being overrun by "idea people." Those staff meeting heroes who've turned their backs on long-term objectives and have opted instead to chase the mythical "silver bullet" concept that solves all of the brand's problems in one fell swoop. It doesn't work that way. There are no shortcuts to brand development.

At best, that so-called antidote equates to the marketing version of a one-hit wonder. Mr. or Ms. Idea may have won the meeting and perhaps the esteem of the high-ranking executive in the room, but the brand just lost. Without company-wide targets to measure against, ideas are nothing more than guesses.

So what's the solution? Discipline. **Don't listen to an idea until you hear an objective.** Whenever an eager thought carrier bursts into your office with the next big thing on the tip of their tongue, stop them and ask:

"What are your objectives?"

That question will act as a filter, allowing on-brand ideas to pass through while eliminating the dangerous off-brand variety. If the person can't tell you what their intentions are, or perhaps offers an agenda incompatible with the company's direction, stop them right there. Don't even listen to the thought. Instead, remind them of your goals and ask that they ensure their concept accomplishes one or all of those aims before presenting again. Adding objectives to the planning process will keep both the team and brand on track.

YEARLY OBJECTIVES WILL KEEP YOU ON TRACK.

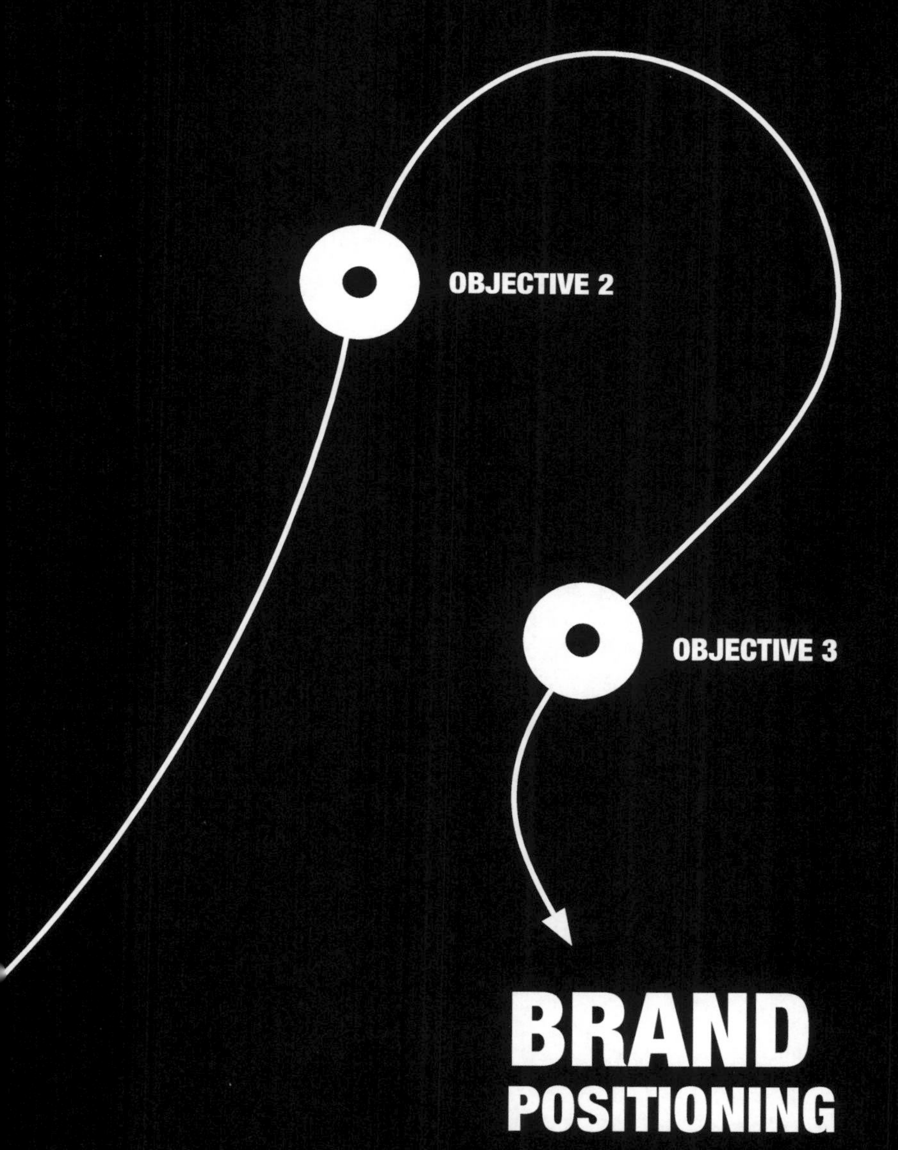

BRAND POSITIONING

HOMEWORK

DATE ....

List three brand objectives that you want to accomplish in the next twelve months.

....

....

....

Note that every objective you outline should come back to and feed into your positioning statement.

HOMEWORK+12

Twelve months after you've completed your initial homework assignment on the preceding pages, come back to this rule and fill out the below to reflect your brand's current state.

DATE ....

List three brand objectives that you want to accomplish in the next twelve months.

....

....

....

IF IT'S NOT ON PAPER, IT'S NOT REAL

RULE #25

Another of my former bosses, and current mentor, once advised, **"If it's not on paper, it's not real."** Meaning if you don't have a documented marketing plan, digital or otherwise, there's nothing to talk about. Stay out of my office. As frustrating as it was at the time, he spoke the truth and taught me a valuable lesson. Without a paper trail, there's nothing to keep a group of free-thinking, idea-chasing marketers on task. Without that documentation to anchor us, planning meetings routinely turned into brainstorms, pushing and pulling the team away from the original strategy and fracturing morale.

Can you build a high-rise without a blueprint? No. Can you build a brand without a formalized plan? No. Marketers are architects of their own kind. Instead of building houses, condos, or commercial real estate, we construct brands. And just like our hotel-designing cousins, without a schematic to follow, we're lost.

But staying on task is not the only reason for putting pen to paper. The exercise itself acts as another brand filter, sifting those employees who follow through on their ideas from those who don't. If you're not willing to put a presentation together to outline your strategy, how can I trust that you'll follow through in executing that strategy?

I can't. And neither could my mentor.

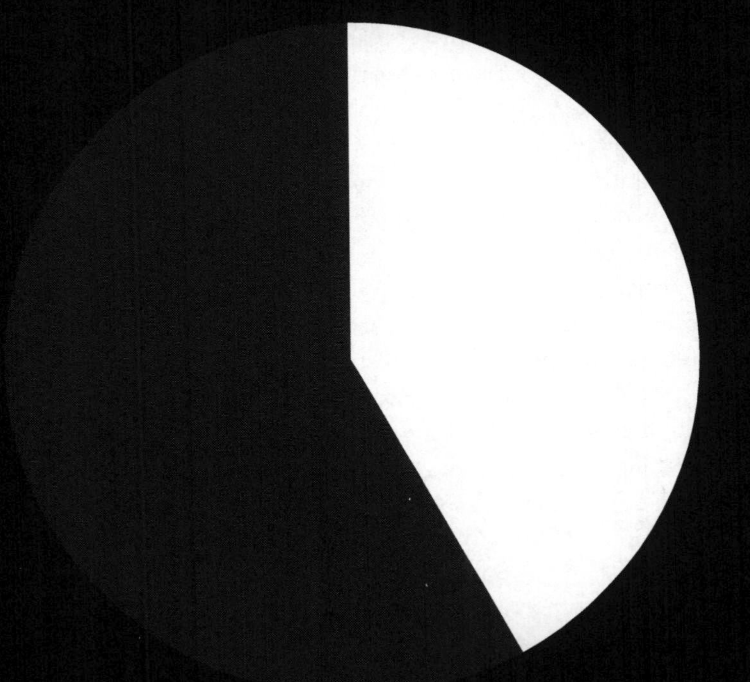

42%

A 2015 STUDY CONDUCTED BY DR. GAIL MATTHEWS, A PSYCHOLOGY PROFESSOR AT DOMINICAN UNIVERSITY OF CALIFORNIA, FOUND THAT PEOPLE ARE 42% MORE LIKELY TO ACCOMPLISH THEIR GOALS BY MERELY WRITING THEM DOWN ON A REGULAR BASIS.

HOMEWORK

Write down the three brand objectives you listed in DARLOW Rule #24.

....

....

....

Write down three strategies you plan to execute in order to accomplish those goals.

HOMEWORK+12

Twelve months after you've completed your initial homework assignment on the preceding pages, come back to this rule and fill out the below to reflect your brand's current state.

DATE ....

Write down the three brand objectives you listed in DARLOW Rule #24.

....

....

....

Write down three strategies you plan to execute in order to accomplish those goals.

NO PLAN

PLAN

GO HOME

RULE #26

When the time comes to build a brand marketing plan, go home. It's not happening at the office. Not with water cooler talk, meeting after meeting, and email jail haunting you from nine a.m. to five p.m. each day.

I learned this lesson (and countless others) while at Ubisoft. It was there that I enjoyed several firsts. I was in my first brand marketing role, as an associate brand manager. I'd been given my first brand to launch and manage on my own, a low-budget first-person-shooter game set in the Wild West by the name of *Call of Juarez*. And it was in that downtown San Francisco building, as an early twentysomething, where I first discovered the power of leaving the office.

The industry had low expectations for *Call of Juarez*; nonetheless, it was my opportunity to prove I belonged, and I wasn't about to take it lightly. But I was running into the same issue many of us face at work: distraction. There was too much happening around me to truly sit down and concentrate on building a launch plan. So I went home to formulate my strategy. That was step one.

Step two was setting the mood. Not only did I need freedom from interruption, but I also needed to immerse myself in the game's narrative. So I hosted my own personal screening of Old West movies. While Billy the Kid did his thing in the background, I channeled my inner sheriff to build one of the strongest marketing plans of my career. It worked.

The game went on to exceed expectations, and I had discovered a solution to planning amid corporate chaos: **go home**.

20%

A fascinating and telling experiment conducted by a group from Carnegie Mellon measured the brainpower lost when a person is interrupted. During the study, 136 participants were asked to read a passage and then answer questions about it. Three separate groups partook in the research. According to the *New York Times* article recapping the results, “One [group] merely completed the test. The other two were told they ‘might be contacted for further instructions’ at any moment.”

During the first test, both the second and third groups, under the expectation that they “might be contacted,” were interrupted twice. In the subsequent test, only the second group was interrupted, while the third group “awaited an interruption that never came.”

The results were powerful, especially in an era of big-box corporations whose offices were lined with desks that offer little to no privacy. The interrupted groups did 20% worse on the questionnaire than members of the distraction-free control group. In the words of the *New York Times*, “The distraction of an interruption, combined with the brain drain of preparing for that interruption, made our test takers 20% dumber.” No doubt a frightening revelation for office dwellers everywhere.

HOMEWORK

Make a list of five places, outside of the office and free of distraction, where you can work on your brand marketing plan.

....

....

....

....

....

Block out one day a week, one day per month, or one day per quarter to work from somewhere other than the office. Write those days down next to the place you plan to work from.

THERE ARE NO PARTICI-PATION AWARDS

RULE #27

They say winning isn't everything. To which I ask, what else is there? If you're not waking up determined to defeat the competition, what's dragging you into work every morning? The paycheck? I hope not. If it's about the money, your brand won't have heart. Is it job security? Better not be. If you're afraid to rock the boat, you're definitely not taking any risks. No heart, no risk, no future.

Marketing is your sport now. You're Larry Bird, and the competition is Magic Johnson. If you want the market share, the money, and the fame, you have to get through Magic and his Lakers first. Bird knew it. While other athletes were out partying, Bird was planning. He became obsessed with beating his former college rival: "The first thing I would do every morning is look at the box scores to see what Magic did. I didn't care about anything else." That obsession to be the best led the former Boston Celtics legend to twelve All-Star appearances, three most valuable player awards, and three championships, including one over Magic and the Lakers in the 1984 NBA Finals. Find your Magic and allow yourself to become obsessed with beating him, her, or it. You and the brand you manage will be better for it.

There are no participation awards. If you're not winning, you're losing, and if you're losing, you won't last.

A STUDY BY NEW YORK UNIVERSITY ASSOCIATE PROFESSOR GAVIN KILDUFF FOUND THAT THE MERE PRESENCE OF AN EQUALLY CAPABLE RACING RIVAL INCREASED A RUNNER'S SPEED BY NEARLY 5 SECONDS PER KILOMETER. A STAT THAT EVERY MARKETER CAN RELATE TO.

MOST OF US ARE BATTLING TO KEEP UP WITH BRANDS BIGGER, STRONGER, AND FASTER THAN OUR OWN. BUT IT'S ONLY THOSE OBSESSED WITH BESTING THOSE RIVALS WHO ACTUALLY WILL.

HOMEWORK

DATE ....

Make a list of the competitors your brand is contending with.

DIRECT COMPETITORS: The rivals most closely resembling your brand and product offering.

BRAND ....
BRAND ....
BRAND ....
BRAND ....
BRAND ....
BRAND ....
BRAND ....

AAA COMPETITION: Of your direct competition, these are the brands considered to be elite (this should be a smaller list).

BRAND ....
BRAND ....
BRAND ....
BRAND ....

OTHER THREATS: Brands outside of your industry who are making an impact and impression on your target audience.

BRAND ....

BRAND ....

BRAND ....

BRAND ....

BRAND ....

BRAND ....

BRAND ....

BRAND ....

BRAND ....

BRAND ....

BRAND ....

BRAND ....

BRAND ....

BRAND ....

HOMEWORK+12

Twelve months after you've completed your initial homework assignment on the preceding pages, come back to this rule and fill out the below to reflect your brand's current state.

DATE ....

Make a list of the competitors your brand is contending with.

DIRECT COMPETITORS: The rivals most closely resembling your brand and product offering.

BRAND ....
BRAND ....
BRAND ....
BRAND ....
BRAND ....

AAA COMPETITION: Of your direct competition, these are the brands considered to be elite (this should be a smaller list).

BRAND ....
BRAND ....
BRAND ....
BRAND ....
BRAND ....

OTHER THREATS: Brands outside of your industry who are making an impact and impression on your target audience.

BRAND ....
BRAND ....
BRAND ....
BRAND ....
BRAND ....
BRAND ....
BRAND ....
BRAND ....
BRAND ....
BRAND ....
BRAND ....
BRAND ....
BRAND ....

KILL OR BE KILLED

RULE #28

You're in a boxing ring, tucked away in one corner. You see your opponent in the other corner, a longtime and heavily favored rival. This is the moment you've been training for—a chance to defeat your competition once and for all.

The bell sounds and the fight begins. You land a jab; they land a jab. You miss on a right hook; they land a left. And another. And another. You're dazed but still standing. Round one ends with you sporting a swollen eye and bruised ego. The crowd is on their side. Things look bleak.

Round two picks up where round one left off. You're getting the worst of this fight—until you see an opening. The body is vulnerable. You pounce. Left. Right. Right. Left. They're not ready for it, and just as they lower their guard to protect the middle and expose their head . . . *WHAM.* You land a fierce uppercut to the jaw. Your opponent's legs are wobbly; with one more shot, this fight will be finished and you'll be the new champion. What do you do?

Before you answer, imagine your opponent is a competing brand, one that's fallen on tough financial times but still holds a significant amount of market share. They're vulnerable. If you overinvest now, there's a good chance you can take that market share away and end their reign. It's **kill or be killed** time; what do you do? Do you get conservative and hope that they throw in the towel? Or do you attack by pouring money into an ad campaign that exposes their weaknesses for the world to see? I know what I would do.

WHAM.

“IF THE
COMPETITION
IS KEEN, I’M WONDERING,

‘WHAT AM I GOING TO DO
TO THIS CHARACTER TO
PSYCHOLOGICALLY
OR PHYSICALLY
DESTROY
HIM?’ ”

—STEVE PREFONTAINE

HOMEWORK

DATE ....

Make a list of the competitors perceived to be stronger than your own brand.

COMPETITOR ....
COMPETITOR ....
COMPETITOR ....
COMPETITOR ....
COMPETITOR ....
COMPETITOR ....
COMPETITOR ....
COMPETITOR ....
COMPETITOR ....
COMPETITOR ....
COMPETITOR ....
COMPETITOR ....
COMPETITOR ....
COMPETITOR ....
COMPETITOR ....

In what areas do these brands struggle?

COMPETITOR ....
VULNERABILITY ....
VULNERABILITY ....
VULNERABILITY ....

COMPETITOR ....
VULNERABILITY ....
VULNERABILITY ....
VULNERABILITY ....

COMPETITOR ....
VULNERABILITY ....
VULNERABILITY ....
VULNERABILITY ....

COMPETITOR ....
VULNERABILITY ....
VULNERABILITY ....
VULNERABILITY ....

Does your brand excel in any of these areas? If yes, circle them.

NOW, ATTACK.

HOMEWORK+12

Twelve months after you've completed your initial homework assignment on the preceding pages, come back to this rule and fill out the below to reflect your brand's current state.

DATE ....

Make a list of the competitors perceived to be stronger than your own brand.

COMPETITOR ....
COMPETITOR ....
COMPETITOR ....
COMPETITOR ....
COMPETITOR ....
COMPETITOR ....
COMPETITOR ....
COMPETITOR ....
COMPETITOR ....
COMPETITOR ....
COMPETITOR ....

In what areas do these brands struggle?

COMPETITOR ....
VULNERABILITY ....
VULNERABILITY ....
VULNERABILITY ....

COMPETITOR ....
VULNERABILITY ....
VULNERABILITY ....
VULNERABILITY ....

COMPETITOR ....
VULNERABILITY ....
VULNERABILITY ....
VULNERABILITY ....

COMPETITOR ....
VULNERABILITY ....
VULNERABILITY ....
VULNERABILITY ....

Does your brand excel in any of these areas? If yes, circle them.

NOW, ATTACK.

YOU LOSE 100% OF THE FIGHTS YOU DON'T PICK

RULE #29

There's so much for marketers to learn from the story of David and Goliath. Not least of which is the fact that David only exists in our world because he convinced his heavily favored adversary to take the fight in the first place. By doing so, David gained instant recognition and fame that, thanks to his ultimate victory, has withstood the test of time. That's the kind of longevity that every brand strives for.

But there's more to be gained from picking a fight than simply brand awareness. Namely, share of voice, defined by Sprout Social as "the amount of the conversation your brand owns with your target audience compared to your competitors."

In a typical boxing match, only two people matter: the two participants squaring off in the middle of the ring. When the bell sounds and the battle starts, all eyes are pointing in the same direction. By picking a fight, a challenger brand creates a natural focal point for consumers to center on—one that cleverly removes the rest of the competition from the conversation while putting a much larger spotlight on the upstart itself. In an instant, the once overlooked brand has been elevated to the market leader's level, shut out the rest of the competition, soaked up any available share of voice, and given itself a chance to dethrone the champion. None of which happens without first convincing the biggest, baddest brand in the bar to step outside.

They say you miss 100% of the shots you don't take. As a challenger brand, **you lose 100% of the fights you don't pick**.

ACCORDING TO NIELSEN, "ALL THINGS BEING EQUAL, A BRAND WHOSE SHARE OF VOICE IS GREATER THAN ITS SHARE OF MARKET IS MORE LIKELY TO GAIN MARKET SHARE."

ONE WAY TO STEAL SHARE OF VOICE AWAY FROM YOUR COMPETITION? PICK A FIGHT.

HOMEWORK

DATE ....

List the competitors perceived to be stronger than your own brand (from the homework section of DARLOW Rule #28).

These are the brands worth picking a fight with.

HOMEWORK+6

Six months after you've completed your homework assignment on the preceding pages, come back to this rule and fill out the below to reflect your brand's current state.

DATE ....

Make a list of the competitors perceived to be stronger than your own brand (from the homework section of DARLOW Rule #28).

These are the brands worth picking a fight with.

DON'T TAKE THE BAIT

RULE #30

If you're a market leader, challenger brands are coming for you. And when they do, **don't take the bait**. It's a trap. Public brand clashes are lose-lose situations for industry favorites and win-wins for the underdog. Starbucks has little to gain from a scuffle with a local coffeehouse. Amazon can't win a war of words with a mom-and-pop bookstore. When you're on top of the mountain, there's only one way you can go: down.

Brand battles like these play out much like they do in sports. When a traditional college football powerhouse like the University of Michigan beats a smaller school, they receive no credit for the victory. But when the opposite happens and Michigan unexpectedly loses to one of those heavy underdogs, all hell breaks loose. That was the case in 2007, when number-five-ranked Michigan, a 33-point favorite, hosted small school Appalachian State and lost.

The media's reaction was relentless in its criticism of the slayed giant from Ann Arbor. *Sports Illustrated* called it "the greatest upset of them all," while Pat Forde of ESPN.com claimed the game was "the most astonishing college football result I can remember."

The reality is that Michigan had nothing to gain and everything to lose that day. A win over an opponent perceived to be far inferior would have generated little for the program. On the other hand, the Mountaineers of Appalachian State, college football's version of a challenger brand, reveled in its newfound attention, enjoying a 15% increase in applications to the school and a 26% jump in ticket sales for all sports between 2007 and 2008.

The underdog laid a trap, and the favorite stepped in it. Don't make the same mistake.

"DO NOT SWALLOW BAIT OFFERED BY THE ENEMY."

—SUN TZU

HOMEWORK

DATE ....

Make a list of the competitors perceived to be weaker than your own brand.

These are the brands to avoid fighting with.

HOMEWORK+6

Six months after you've completed your homework assignment on the preceding pages, come back to this rule and fill out the below to reflect your brand's current state.

DATE ....

Make a list of the competitors perceived to be weaker than your own brand.

These are the brands to avoid fighting with.

TALK WHEN THEY'RE NOT

RULE #31

I'm about to let you in on a dirty little marketing secret: brand managers love to recycle certain elements of their marketing plans, one of the most common being advertising cadence. The weeks and months a company invests to promote their product will often carry over from one year to the next. All you have to do is track their rhythms for twelve months, and you'll know their playbook for the next eighteen to twenty-four.

The question is, what do you do with this information? That's easy, **talk when they're not**. If I know the industry is prone to heavy up its advertising during the months of November and December but will predictably remain dark from July to October, guess when I'm investing money to build the brand? July to October.

Three things happen when you spend on brand communication during months in which the competition is quiet. First, you own a much larger share of voice. Less noise from competitors means more attention paid to your brand message.

Second, by talking for weeks in a room free of opposition, you've given yourself a head start at building relationships. From July to October, you'll have formed deep-rooted bonds with potential consumers without interference from competing agendas.

Finally, it's cheaper. The fewer companies bidding on advertising space, the more affordable it is for you to buy. All of which means that while your competition opts to reprise last year's media plan to save time, you'll be using that knowledge to quietly grow your share of voice, build brand loyalty, and steal market share out from under them at a discounted rate.

But I'm not one to gossip, so you didn't hear that from me.

IN WHICH ROOM WILL IT BE EASIER
TO HEAR AND BE HEARD?

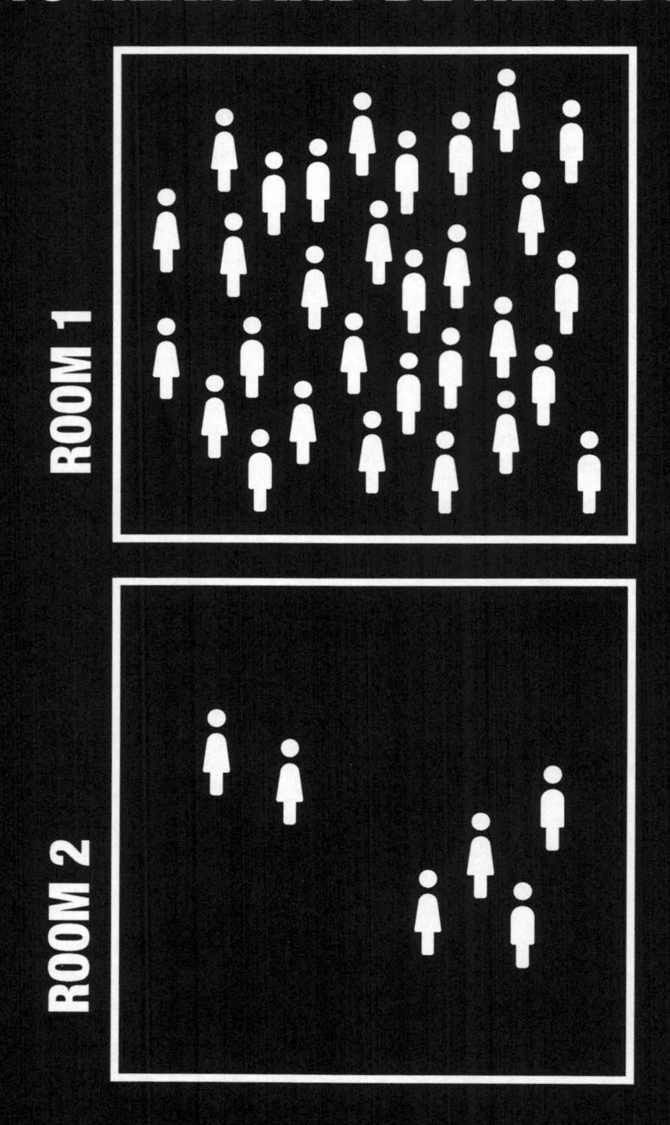

If you've ever tried to hold a conversation in a crowded bar, you know how difficult it can be. The louder the room gets, the louder people talk, all in an effort to be heard. Advertising is no different. The more competition you have speaking (a.k.a. advertising) at the same time, the harder and more expensive it is for your consumer to hear you. If you're like most companies, you can't afford the investment necessary to win this decibel battle. So what's the alternative?

Here's an idea: instead of straining to compete in that crowded brand bar during peak season, wait until the off-season. While the audience may be smaller, the wine flows deeper, the conversations are richer, and most importantly, it's easier to hear.

HOMEWORK

1. Create a line graph visualizing when and how much your brand is communicating throughout the year.

    X AXIS: Months of the Year
    Y AXIS: Scale of 1–10 "AMOUNT OF BRAND PROMOTION"

2. Using a different color each time, do the same for every direct competitor.

3. Make a note of the months in which your competition is light on brand communication.

Now talk when they're not.

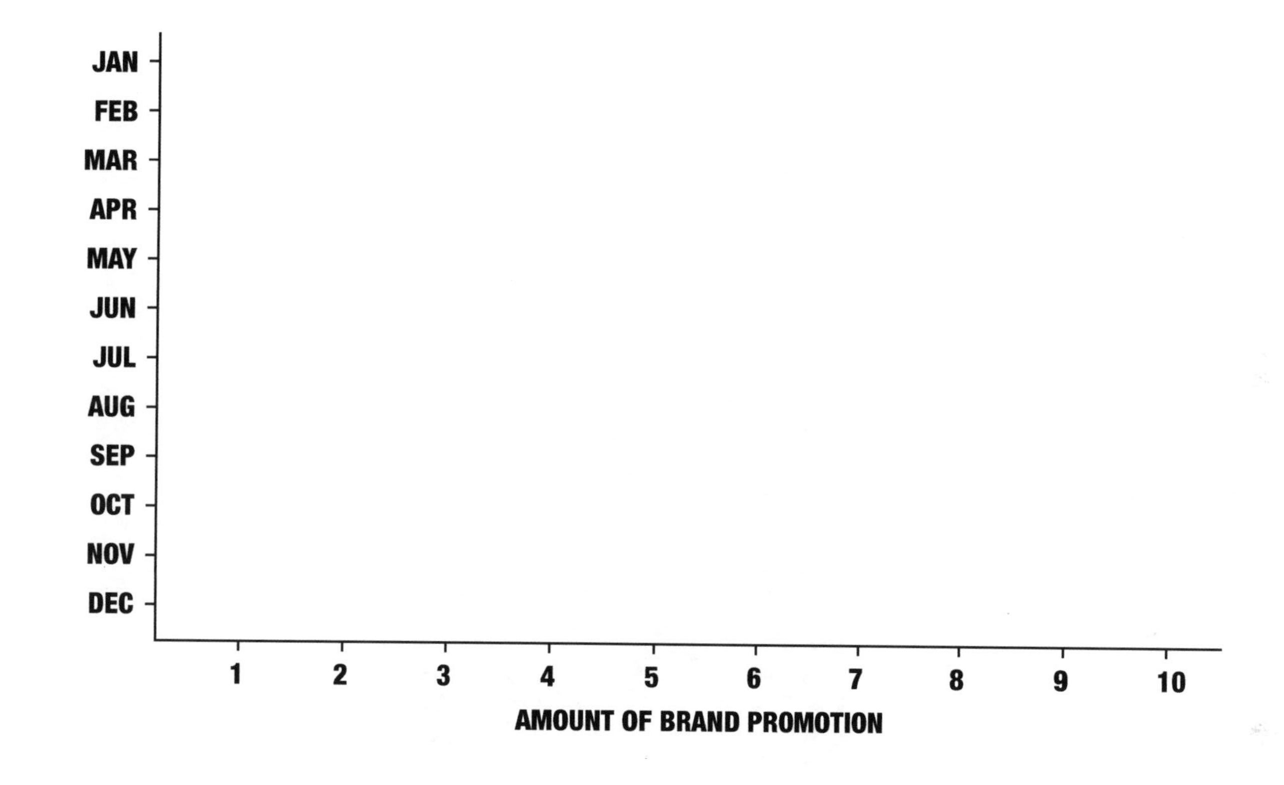
JAN
FEB
MAR
APR
MAY
JUN
JUL
AUG
SEP
OCT
NOV
DEC
1
2
3
4
5
6
7
8
9
10
AMOUNT OF BRAND PROMOTION

QUALITY OVER QUANTITY

RULE #32

When it comes to building a social media community, quality beats quantity. Having thousands of Instagram followers only matters if they're the right followers: people who believe in and are fanatical enough about your brand message to repeat it back to you and engage, much like at a concert.

Choosing **quality over quantity** is the difference between an arena packed with die-hard fans of your music stomping, clapping, and singing your songs in unison versus a lethargic, unenthusiastic crowd waiting for the next band to come onstage.

A big gathering does you no good if those in attendance don't enjoy your genre of music. The more like-minded and passionate your audience is about your brand, the stronger it'll appear and feel to the outside world. That leads to more of the right fans, more of the right headlines, and more of the right buzz.

Instead of spending your time trying to sell out Madison Square Garden for the sake of saying you did, turn your attention to packing that intimate club down the street with people who want to be there.

YES

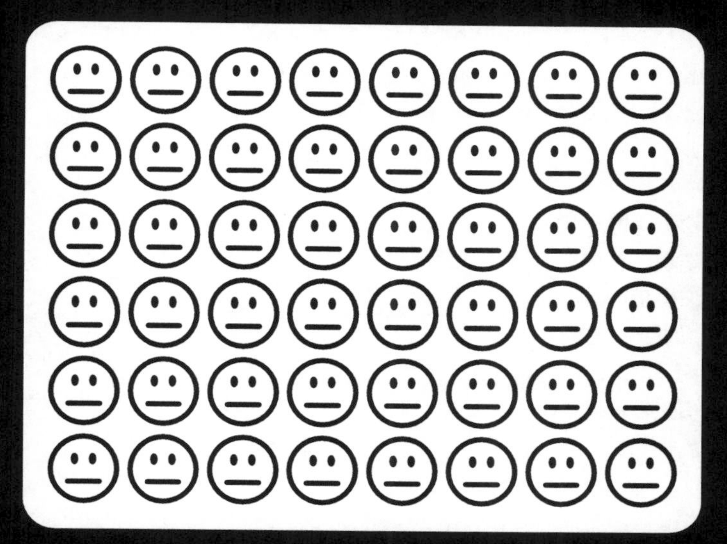

NO

HOMEWORK

Describe your primary, secondary, and tertiary consumer segments in as much detail as possible. Go beyond the suggested descriptors below.

PRIMARY CONSUMER: The consumers most important to the success of your brand, oftentimes your most engaged, high-volume purchasers.

AGE RANGE ....

GENDER ....

GEOGRAPHIC LOCATION ....

EDUCATION ....

OCCUPATION ....

INTERESTS ....

PERSONALITY TRAITS ....

VALUES ....

SECONDARY CONSUMER: An important community that buys and engages with your brand but not quite at the level of or for the same reasons as the primary group. This may also be a segment that is influential to your primary consumer, making them critical to your brand communication strategy and ultimate success.

AGE RANGE ....
GENDER ....
GEOGRAPHIC LOCATION ....
EDUCATION ....
OCCUPATION ....
INTERESTS ....
PERSONALITY TRAITS ....
VALUES ....

TERTIARY CONSUMER: A group who, as of today, does not affect direct sales but may in the future. Similar to your secondary consumer, this may also be a group that influences one of your other target consumer sets.

AGE RANGE ....
GENDER ....
GEOGRAPHIC LOCATION ....
EDUCATION ....
OCCUPATION ....
INTERESTS ....
PERSONALITY TRAITS ....
VALUES ....

BRAND MARKET-ING IS ABOUT EMPATHY

RULE #33

Research shows that 40 million adults suffer from anxiety in the United States, while 14.8 million people deal with depression. Now in my own estimation, that means there are over 40 million potentially great brand marketers living in America. Why do I say that? Because **brand marketing is about empathy**. The ability to recognize that life is hard, Facebook profiles are curated, and no one, not even Beyoncé, is perfect is the key to your success. People struggle, and the more you, the marketer, can relate to that struggle, the better at building a brand you'll be.

So stop pretending your brand is spotless and life is flawless. Neither is true. Neither is relatable. Your product is here to help repair a small part of our fragile psyches. I didn't ask Santa for the Dee Brown Reebok Pump basketball shoes as a kid because I thought they would make me a better point guard. I had to have them because they looked cool, all of my friends wanted them, and in my head, that combination added up to girls liking me. Humans are a simple species. We're thinking at the surface and managing our delicate egos, just like you.

That's why your own struggle as a person is your superpower as a marketer. You get it. You get me. You get us. You know the real reason people buy what they buy, and it's not because that $10,000 Rolex watch is great at telling time.

"YOU NEVER REALLY
UNDERSTAND
A PERSON
UNTIL YOU CONSIDER THINGS FROM
HIS POINT OF VIEW—
UNTIL YOU CLIMB INTO HIS SKIN
AND WALK AROUND IN IT."

—HARPER LEE

HOMEWORK

1. List the areas of your life in which you struggle (top circle).

2. List the presumed areas of struggle in your target consumer's life (bottom circle).

3. List those struggles found under both your life and your target consumer's life (middle space where the circles intersect).

4. Highlight those common struggles that your brand can authentically offer relief or support for.

Those highlighted areas are spaces in which you will have the strongest understanding, the empathy necessary, and the means as a brand to solve.

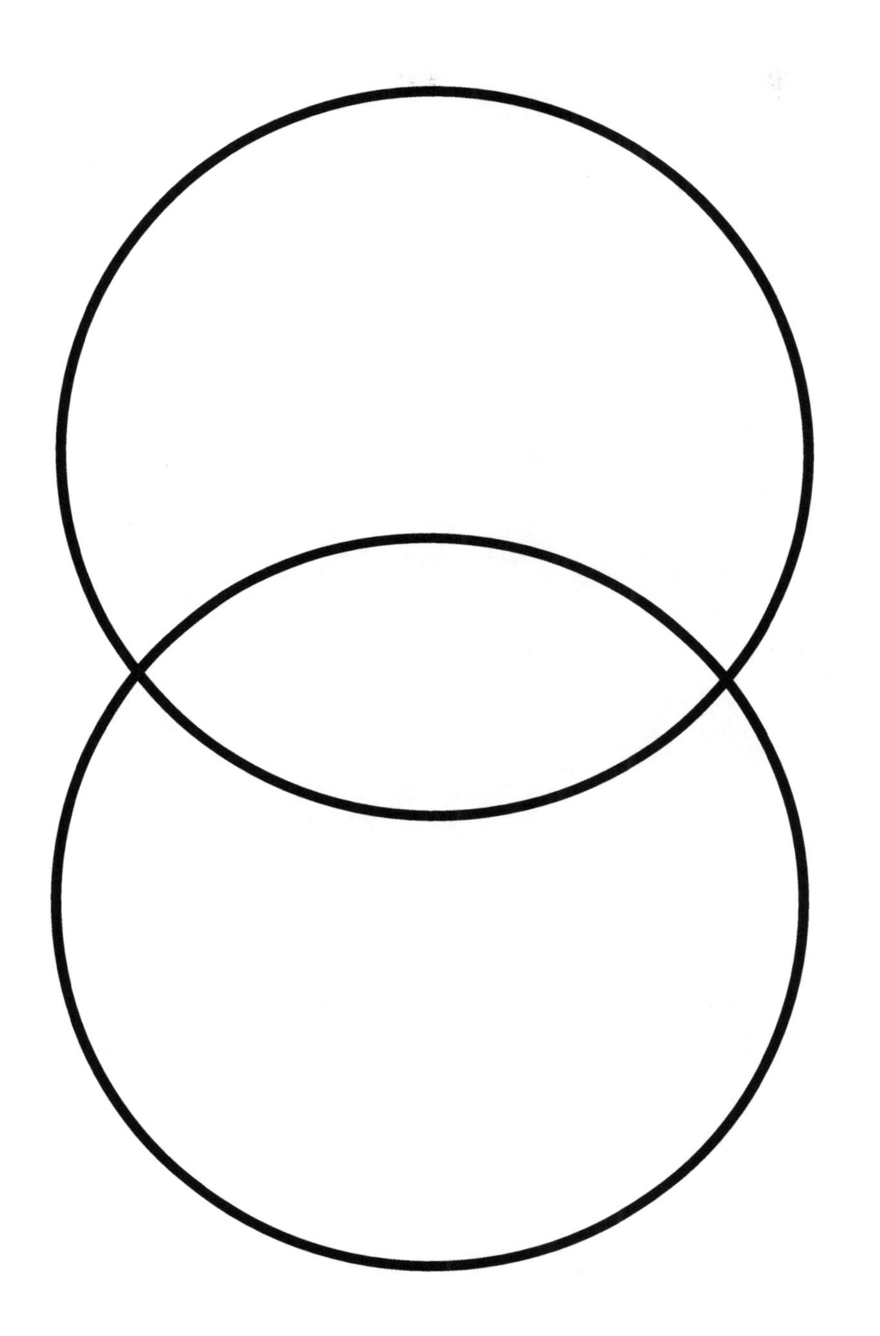

"ONLY IF WE
UNDERSTAND
CAN WE
CARE.
ONLY IF WE
CARE
WILL WE
HELP."

—JANE GOODALL

NOT ALL INFLUENCE IS CREATED EQUAL

RULE #34

Sitting in a trendy Brooklyn bookstore one day, surrounded by "cool kids," I found myself inspired. As I quietly observed a community of so-called hipsters, it became clear to me that **not all influence is created equal**.

You're not cool because you choose to wear dirty sweatpants, shoes your dad wore in the 1980s, and a frayed beanie that's less than stellar at keeping your head warm. And you're not cool because you've opted for ramen noodle dinners and broken water heaters rather than using your education to land a well-paying job working for the Man. Or are you?

What I realized that day is that the answer is yes *and* no. To some, embracing "the struggle" is admirable, positioning the person going through tough times as an influencer to a particular community. To others, the high-ranking executive working for a corporate giant and driving a gas-guzzling sports car is admirable, making that person an influencer. The truth is that everyone is persuasive at some level and to someone.

The hard part isn't finding influencers; the hard part is finding *your* influencers. While an appearance by professional baseball player Mike Trout at a high school baseball game has the power to change teenage lives, Trout could walk into that same chic Brooklyn bookstore wearing his game jersey, with his face covered in eye black, while holding a baseball bat, and no one would look twice. He's not their hero. If that's your audience, no matter how many home runs he's hit, he's not your influencer. Keep looking.

ONE PERSON'S "STUPIDITY" . . .

"BRITAIN'S BEST-LOVED ARTWORK IS A BANKSY. THAT'S PROOF OF OUR STUPIDITY."

—JONATHAN JONES IN *THE GUARDIAN*

. . . IS ANOTHER PERSON'S "BRILLIANCE."

"BANKSY'S SHREDDED PAINTING WAS A MOMENT OF CREATIVE BRILLIANCE."

—JOSH LINKNER, *DETROIT FREE PRESS*

HOMEWORK

1. List the people deemed influential to your primary consumer (top circle).

2. List the people deemed influential to your secondary consumer (bottom circle).

3. List the individuals listed under both (middle space where the circles intersect).

Start by partnering with and seeding your product to the personalities common to both consumer groups.

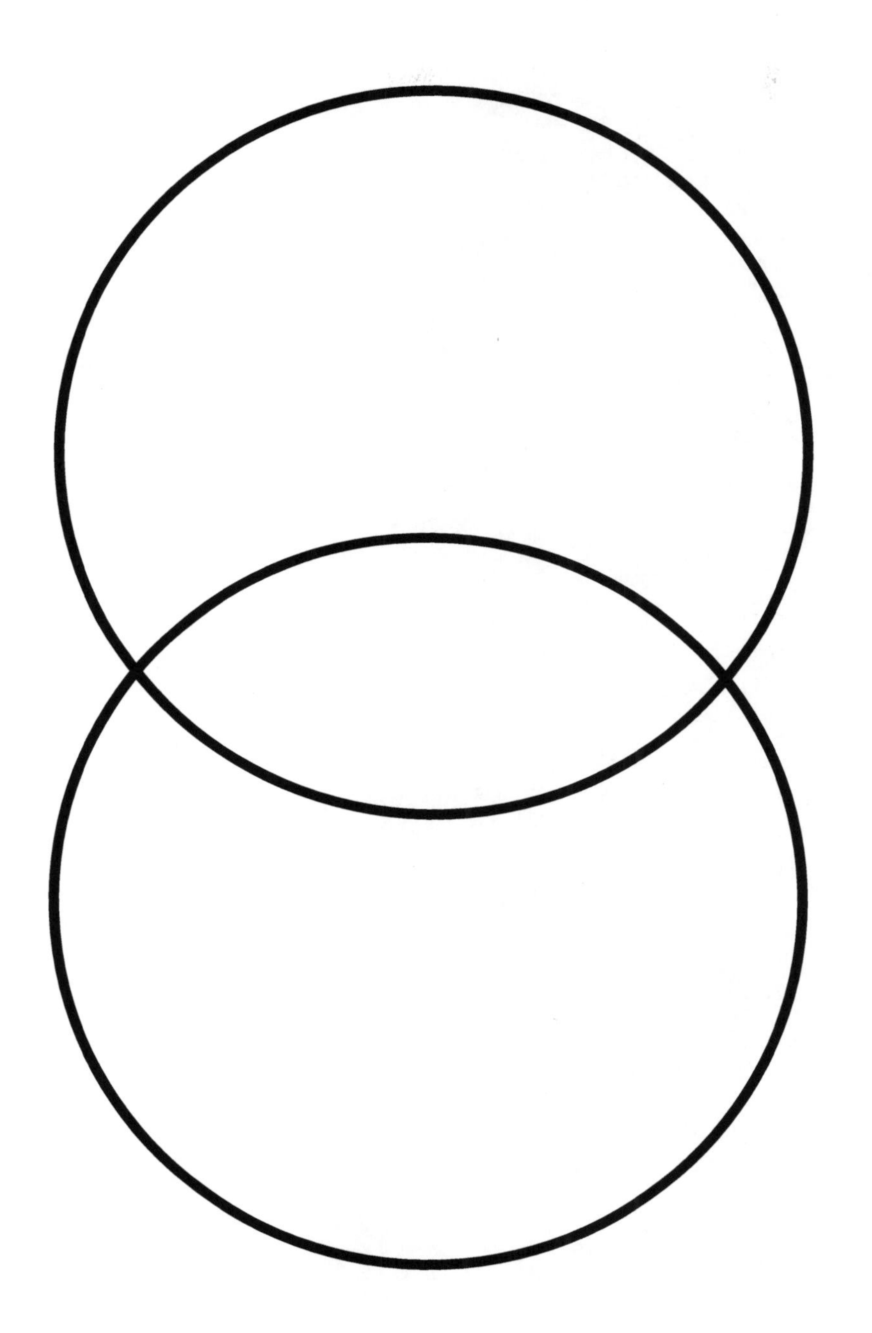

GIVE YOUR AUDIENCE WHAT THEY WANT, NOT WHAT YOU NEED

RULE #35

Does it make sense to serve your consumers content they're not interested in? Of course not. So quit spamming them. Just because someone loves beer doesn't mean they love all beer. Just because someone listens to music doesn't mean they want to know about every album release. And just because someone bought one of your products doesn't mean they want the rest of them. Whether it's through social media, direct mail, or email, give your consumers what they want, when they want it, or risk losing them.

And that, ladies and gentlemen, is today's marketplace. The consumer has the leverage, not you. You're expendable. Fifty years ago, lack of choice funneled all of the power to the handful of options that existed in a given industry. Today if you're not delivering precisely what the consumer needs, someone else will, and fast.

Beer geeks are not interested in deals on Coors Light, so stop tweeting about it or they'll unfollow you and follow someone else instead. Fans of punk rock don't care about Adele's latest album, so stop sending emails about it or they'll unsubscribe from you and subscribe to someone who gets them. If your brand serves multiple audiences, having a single channel to communicate from might be easier for you, but it's a bad experience for your consumer. And that's what matters. **Give your audience what they want, not what you need.**

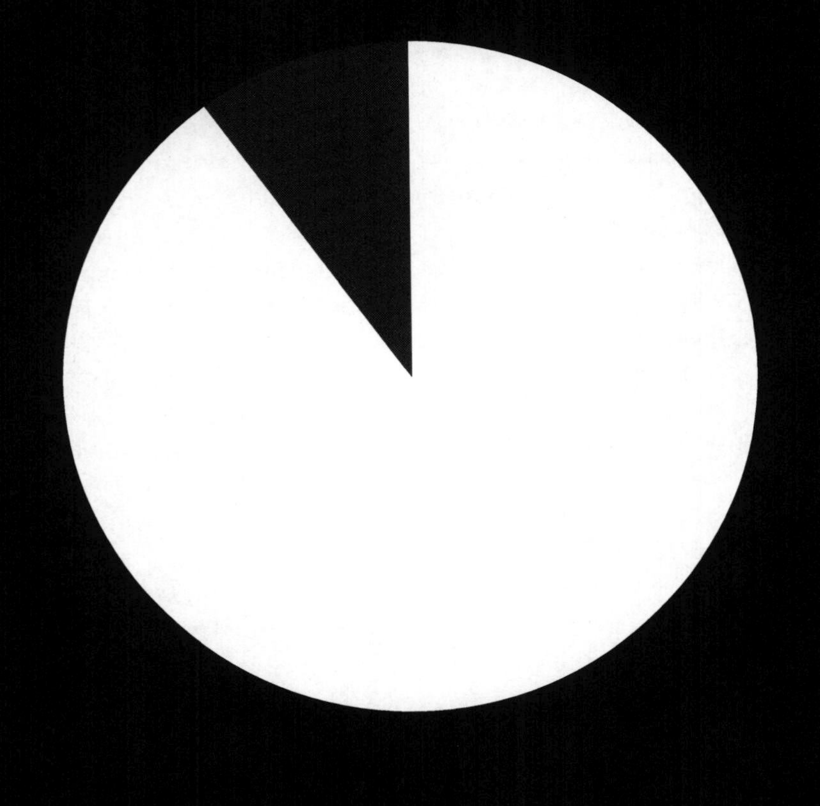

90%

ACCORDING TO A 2017 SURVEY PUBLISHED BY STATISTA, OUT OF A GROUP OF ONE THOUSAND ADULTS FROM THE UNITED STATES, 90% FOUND PERSONALIZED CONTENT VERY OR SOMEWHAT APPEALING.

HOMEWORK

Note that while your brand position does not change, the messages you choose to emphasize within that position may vary by audience.

For example, while my personal position as the "marketing executive helping college athletes, coaches, and teams build their brands" stays the same, my message to each consumer group differs. When communicating with coaches, I may focus on my experience working with some of the biggest college sports brands in the country, including programs like Notre Dame, UCLA, and the University of Miami. Or perhaps I could choose to emphasize my first book (*Brands Win Championships*), which teaches readers how to build successful team brands through marketing. Each is relevant to a coach.

Conversely, when talking to athletes, I may decide to play up my history of developing communication strategies for well-known sports and entertainment brands like Aaron Rodgers, Kris Bryant, and Kanye West. Or I might opt to highlight my second book (*Athletes Are Brands Too*), which is dedicated to teaching athletes how to build a personal brand that reaches beyond the court or field. In each case, I am reinforcing my personal brand position, but I'm doing so with messages and tools unique and specific to my differing target consumers.

Using the chart on the following pages, fill in the information below for each of your target consumer segments.

CONSUMER SEGMENT

Use the target consumer segments defined in DARLOW Rule #32.

BRAND MESSAGE

What brand message are you delivering to each individual consumer group?

CONSUMER TAKEAWAY

What is the intended consumer takeaway from each message?

COMMUNICATION PLATFORM(S)

What communication platform(s) will you use to deliver these messages?

HOMEWORK

CONSUMER SEGMENT	BRAND MESSAGE

CONSUMER TAKEAWAY	COMMUNICATION PLATFORM(S)

IT'S NOT A BRAND'S JOB TO MAKE EVERY-ONE HAPPY

RULE #36

There's a disease infecting weak, insecure brands all over the world. It's called "all things to all people" syndrome. Symptoms include trend chasing, erratic brand identity, and inconsistent messaging. There is only one known cure: self-assurance.

If you believe in your brand, others will too—but not everyone. So stop worrying about your perfect record, and just build the best brand you can. Achieving a 100% approval rate is an impossible task. It doesn't matter how great you think your product or brand is; you're not making everyone happy. Ever.

Look at it this way: there are people in this world who dislike drinking *water*. Without water, there are no people. Yet even the H_2O brand has its detractors. I don't know what you're selling, but it's not as important as water. Quit trying to be.

It's not a brand's job to make everyone happy; it's a brand's job to make *some* people *very* happy.

HOW TO BUILD A FOLLOWING

PERSON DOESN'T LIKE YOUR BRAND:

PERSON LIKES YOUR BRAND:

HOMEWORK

WHO LOVES YOU: What types of consumers do you anticipate loving your brand or have already proven to love your brand?

WHO HATES YOU: What types of consumers do you anticipate hating your brand or have already proven to dislike your brand? Oftentimes, these groups are the antithesis of the groups who love you or are supporters of your direct competitors.

Knowing and planning for the fact that not everyone will admire your brand is powerful knowledge that you can use to further engage the fans that do appreciate you.

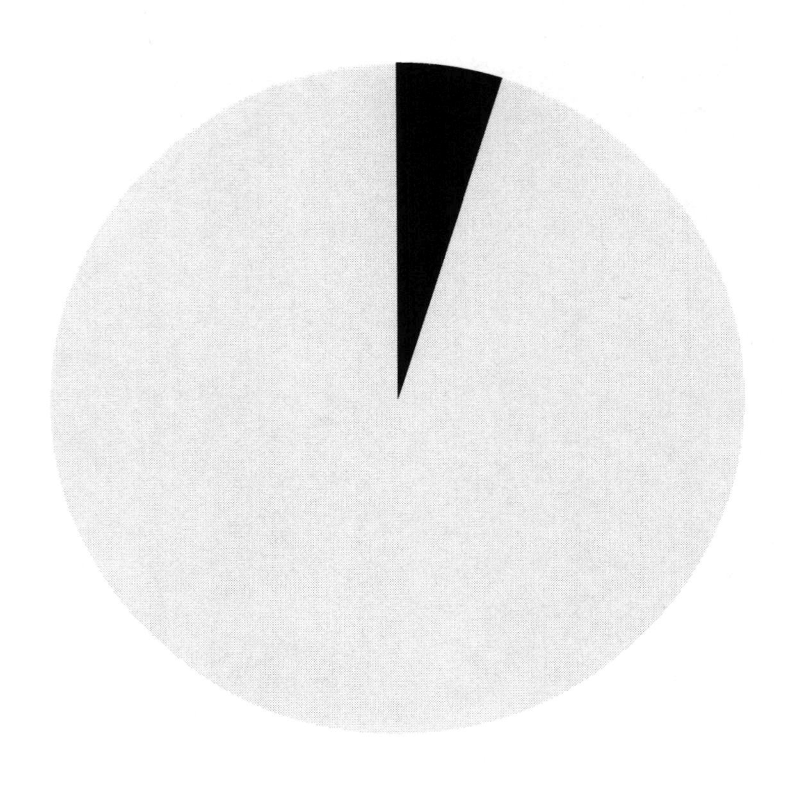

5%

ACCORDING TO AN ARTICLE BY THE *HARVARD BUSINESS REVIEW*, BASED ON ORIGINAL RESEARCH DONE BY FREDERICK REICHHELD OF BAIN & COMPANY, "INCREASING CUSTOMER RETENTION RATES BY 5% INCREASES PROFITS BY 25% TO 95%."

STOP WASTING YOUR TIME TRYING TO CONVINCE PEOPLE WHO DISLIKE YOUR BRAND TO CHANGE THEIR MINDS. INSTEAD, TURN THE CONSUMERS WHO LIKE YOU INTO CONSUMERS WHO LOVE YOU.

KILL INDIFFER-ENCE

RULE #37

When consumers hear your brand's name, what do they feel? Is it love? Is it hate? If the answer is indifference, you're failing. Marketing is about eliciting reactions and emotion from a targeted audience. If your community lives somewhere in the middle, shrugging their shoulders at the sight and sound of your name, something is wrong, and the brand is almost certainly void of significant press coverage.

That being said, it's not easy to adopt such a polarizing stance on brand management. Criticism stings, hate is terrifying, and science suggests negativity is hard for humans to come back from. According to Scott Mautz in *Inc.*, "It takes our brain experiencing five positive events to make up for the psychological effect of just one negative event." Yet even within that built-in emotional doom and gloom, there is opportunity to zig when everyone else is zagging. While most run from disparagement, the brands who **kill indifference** shine.

The media doesn't care which way the needle moves as long as it's moving. So while the feeble hide in the corner, satisfied with neither winning nor losing, the brands that deliver polarizing stories routinely find themselves on the front pages of the blogs and news sites that matter. You know the ultra-popular outlets I'm talking about—the ones that half the country loves and half the country hates.

Imagine that.

Love me or hate me, but *feel* me.

"I WANT YOU TO FEEL
REPULSED
OR
EXHILARARATED."

—ALEXANDER MCQUEEN

HOMEWORK

Why do people love your brand?

Why do people hate your brand?

Use this information to build a communication strategy that simultaneously pulls in the people who love you and pushes away the people who don't.

WITHOUT HATE, THERE IS NO LOVE

RULE #38

The more people hate your brand, the more people love your brand. That might sound counterintuitive, and at some point, in a history littered with scarcity, it may have been. But in today's plentiful world, where we have the luxury of "picking a side," hate for one company or product is often born out of love for another. People have become programmed to choose teams, and if your brand sits on the other side of the river, guess what? We don't like you. But that can be a good thing, because as Newton hypothesized, for every action, there is an equal and opposite reaction. While one group tears your brand down, another will build it up. While your detractors criticize your every move, your fans will come to your defense. And with each confrontation, that army of supporters becomes more and more invested in and loyal to you.

So the next time you have a chance to feed your trolls, do it. Because **without hate, there is no love**.

“FANS DON’T BOO NOBODIES.”

—REGGIE JACKSON

HOMEWORK

What can you do and/or say to further supporters' love for your brand while simultaneously feeding your naysayers' disdain for it?

DAR
LOW

CONSUMERS ARE MASOCHISTS

RULE #39

Make your consumers wait in long lines. Piss them off when your site goes down from too much traffic. Disappoint them by limiting the release of your product to the point where it sells out in seconds. They'll love you for it.

Consumers are masochists. We want what we can't have. We want to eat at the restaurant that takes reservations eight months out. We want to get married at the church that's booked for the next ten years. We want to say we were there and you weren't. Until you are, then we're out.

Once the limited-release sneaker becomes available to hundreds of thousands of people, versus the previously exclusive group of one thousand, the allure of the brand is gone. The lines that stretched around the block on launch day are now a thing of the past, and the product itself is dead. You did it wrong. Greed killed your "cool."

Hype comes from antagonizing your audience, and patience is once again the key. You're not just selling a product; you're selling street cred. The moment you succumb to your own short-term financial gains and insatiable ego, oversaturating the market with a once coveted item, the social currency you previously enjoyed disappears, and you lose.

Goodbye lines, farewell traffic, so long sales.

1,417

IN 2013, 1,417 PEOPLE WAITED OUTSIDE THE APPLE FLAGSHIP STORE IN NEW YORK CITY FOR THE LATEST iPHONE RELEASE. PROMOTIONAL PERFECTION. NOTHING BUILDS BRAND PERCEPTION QUITE LIKE A PHOTO OF RABID FANS WAITING IN A LONG LINE TO BUY YOUR PRODUCT.

CONVERSELY, NOTHING KILLS PERCEPTION LIKE AN EMPTY STORE FILLED WITH UNSOLD AND DISCOUNTED MERCHANDISE. WHICH WOULD YOU RATHER HAVE? WHICH DO YOU HAVE?

HOMEWORK

List the products you have or can develop that you would be willing to offer in a limited quantity.

Under each product, name the consumer group most likely to wait in line for said product.

PRODUCT ....
TARGET CONSUMER ....

PRODUCT ....
TARGET CONSUMER ....

PRODUCT ....
TARGET CONSUMER ....

PRODUCT ....
TARGET CONSUMER ....

PRODUCT ....
TARGET CONSUMER ....

PRODUCT ....
TARGET CONSUMER ....

PRODUCT ....
TARGET CONSUMER ....

PRODUCT ....
TARGET CONSUMER ....

PRODUCT ....
TARGET CONSUMER ....

PRODUCT ....
TARGET CONSUMER ....

PRODUCT ....
TARGET CONSUMER ....

PRODUCT ....
TARGET CONSUMER ....

“I DON’T WANT TO BELONG TO ANY CLUB THAT WILL ACCEPT PEOPLE LIKE ME AS A MEMBER.”

—GROUCHO MARX

PEOPLE TRUST PEOPLE, NOT COMPA- NIES

RULE #40

Just because your commercial says your product is great doesn't mean we believe it. What else would you say? It's your product. If you really want to sell consumers on the quality of your latest creation, get other people to say they love it. Find real, everyday shoppers who have actually tried and enjoyed the merchandise. Get those people to spread the word for you. And I have just the mechanism to do it. Are you ready for me to blow your mind? Here goes . . . online reviews. Yeah, sorry it's not a revolutionary concept. That's what makes it great. Whether you're working for a multibillion-dollar global brand (been there) or you're an author trying to make a living writing (still there), reviews have a proven track record of success. According to *Inc.*, 84% of us trust online reviews as much as we trust a personal recommendation.

You know what's better than a television commercial claiming you're the best at what you do? A television commercial claiming you're the best at what you do accompanied by a horde of corroborating five-star reviews. That's because **people trust people, not companies**.

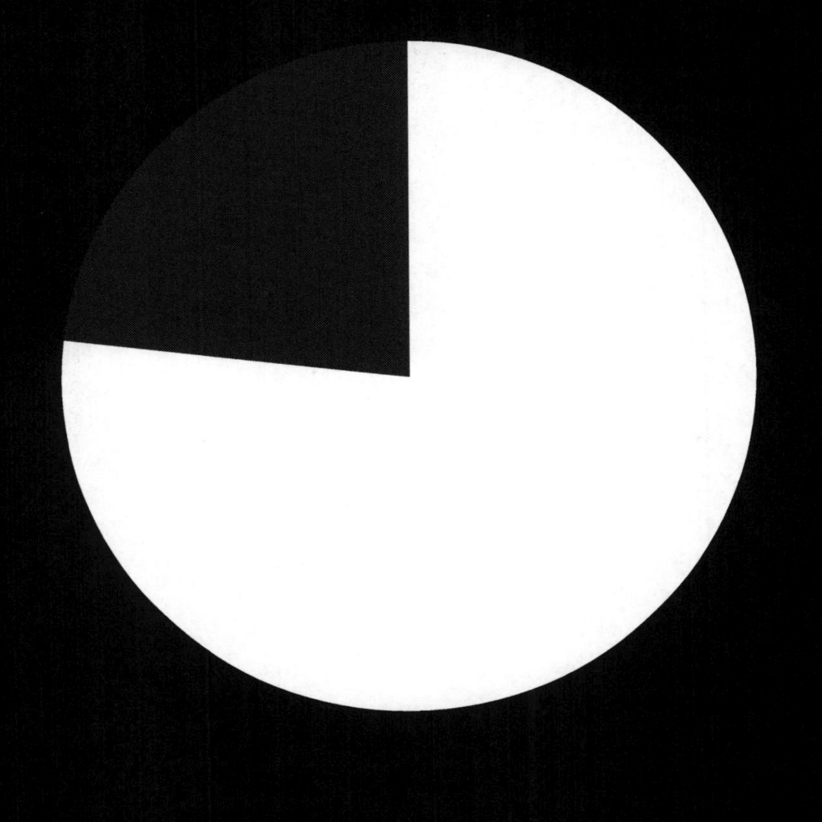

77%

ACCORDING TO *THE DRUM*, 60% OF CONSUMERS LOOK AT ONLINE REVIEWS WEEKLY, WHILE 77% AGREED THAT IF ASKED BY A LOCAL BUSINESS, THEY WOULD LEAVE A REVIEW.

HAVE YOU ASKED?

HOMEWORK

DATE ....

Where is your brand being reviewed?

How many reviews does your brand have in that space?

What is your average review rating in that space?

WHERE ....
NUMBER OF REVIEWS ....
AVERAGE RATING ....

WHERE ....
NUMBER OF REVIEWS ....
AVERAGE RATING ....

WHERE ....
NUMBER OF REVIEWS ....
AVERAGE RATING ....

WHERE ....
NUMBER OF REVIEWS ....
AVERAGE RATING ....

WHERE ....
NUMBER OF REVIEWS ....
AVERAGE RATING ....

WHERE ....
NUMBER OF REVIEWS ....
AVERAGE RATING ....

WHERE ....
NUMBER OF REVIEWS ....
AVERAGE RATING ....

WHERE ....
NUMBER OF REVIEWS ....
AVERAGE RATING ....

WHERE ....
NUMBER OF REVIEWS ....
AVERAGE RATING ....

WHERE ....
NUMBER OF REVIEWS ....
AVERAGE RATING ....

WHERE ....
NUMBER OF REVIEWS ....
AVERAGE RATING ....

Make it a goal to improve upon these numbers over the coming months.

HOMEWORK+3

Three months after you've completed your initial homework assignment on the preceding pages, come back to this rule and fill out the below to reflect your brand's current state.

DATE ....

Where is your brand being reviewed?

How many reviews does your brand have in that space?

What is your average review rating in that space?

WHERE ....
NUMBER OF REVIEWS ....
AVERAGE RATING ....

WHERE ....
NUMBER OF REVIEWS ....
AVERAGE RATING ....

WHERE ....
NUMBER OF REVIEWS ....
AVERAGE RATING ....

WHERE ....
NUMBER OF REVIEWS ....
AVERAGE RATING ....

WHERE ....
NUMBER OF REVIEWS ....
AVERAGE RATING ....

WHERE ....
NUMBER OF REVIEWS ....
AVERAGE RATING ....

WHERE ....
NUMBER OF REVIEWS ....
AVERAGE RATING ....

WHERE ....
NUMBER OF REVIEWS ....
AVERAGE RATING ....

WHERE ....
NUMBER OF REVIEWS ....
AVERAGE RATING ....

WHERE ....
NUMBER OF REVIEWS ....
AVERAGE RATING ....

WHERE ....
NUMBER OF REVIEWS ....
AVERAGE RATING ....

Make it a goal to improve upon these numbers over the coming months.

HOMEWORK+6

Six months after you've completed your HOMEWORK+3 assignment on the preceding pages, come back to this rule and fill out the below to reflect your brand's current state.

DATE ....

Where is your brand being reviewed?

How many reviews does your brand have in that space?

What is your average review rating in that space?

WHERE ....
NUMBER OF REVIEWS ....
AVERAGE RATING ....

WHERE ....
NUMBER OF REVIEWS ....
AVERAGE RATING ....

WHERE ....
NUMBER OF REVIEWS ....
AVERAGE RATING ....

WHERE ....
NUMBER OF REVIEWS ....
AVERAGE RATING ....

WHERE ....

NUMBER OF REVIEWS ....

AVERAGE RATING ....

WHERE ....

NUMBER OF REVIEWS ....

AVERAGE RATING ....

WHERE ....

NUMBER OF REVIEWS ....

AVERAGE RATING ....

WHERE ....

NUMBER OF REVIEWS ....

AVERAGE RATING ....

WHERE ....

NUMBER OF REVIEWS ....

AVERAGE RATING ....

WHERE ....

NUMBER OF REVIEWS ....

AVERAGE RATING ....

WHERE ....

NUMBER OF REVIEWS ....

AVERAGE RATING ....

Make it a goal to improve upon these numbers over the coming months.

YOU ARE THE COMPANY THAT YOU KEEP

RULE #41

If you're not managing your brand like a shallow teenager, you're doing it wrong. Brands are no different than insecure adolescents navigating a high school cafeteria. The table you sit at and the group you sit with establish your position in the social hierarchy. **You are the company that you keep.** Make the wrong choice as a naïve freshman and . . . well, good luck getting invited to that house party. Why don't they teach you that in school? Asking for a friend.

What marketers often fail to recognize is that life after high school is simply an extension of high school itself. As a teenager, reputation is everything. As a brand, perception is reality. Same thing.

Like a teenager's reputation, everything that comes into contact with your brand sticks. That makes decisions, like which companies to collaborate with, critical. Who and what you associate with will affect how your brand is perceived for better or worse. When you partner with another brand, two become one. You take on their good and bad. The cooler they are, the cooler you are. So the next time you walk into that cafeteria, find your way to the coolest table and pick out your new best (brand) friend.

Maybe then you'll get invited to that house party.

COOL BY ASSOCIATION:

ADJ. **ACHIEVING A HIGHER SOCIAL STATUS THROUGH ASSOCIATION WITH A POPULAR PERSON. (URBAN DICTIONARY)**

HOMEWORK

DATE ....

Which brand would you benefit from partnering with?

....

Why would that collaboration help your brand's perception?

....

....

....

....

....

....

....

What type of collaboration would benefit your brand the most?

....

....

....

....

....

....

....

How does the collaboration feed into your brand position?

....

....

....

....

....

....

....

Which of your target consumers would benefit most from the collaboration?

....

....

....

....

....

....

....

NOW REACH OUT.

HOMEWORK+12

Twelve months after you've completed your initial homework assignment on the preceding pages, come back to this rule and fill out the below to reflect your brand's current state.

DATE ....

Which brand would you benefit from partnering with?

....

Why would that collaboration help your brand's perception?

....

....

....

....

....

....

What type of collaboration would benefit your brand the most?

....

....

....

....

....

....

How does the collaboration feed into your brand position?

....

....

....

....

....

....

Which of your target consumers would benefit most from the collaboration?

....

....

....

....

....

....

NOW REACH OUT.

INFLUEN-CERS EXIST, AND YOU NEED THEM

RULE #42

The term *influencer* has become tired and overused (in this book, no less); I understand that. But **influencers exist, and you need them**. The idea that someone can be seen as important because they have a blue check next to their Instagram handle is ridiculous. I understand that too. But that seal of approval brings with it a certain level of credibility that, no matter how absurd we may think it is, affects our opinion of the profile donning it.

According to Social Media Today, influencer marketing delivers eleven times the return on investment that traditional digital marketing does. We know it works. So don't let your ego or the absurdity of social influence get in the way of your brand's growth. Instead, use it to your advantage. Identify the thought leaders in your community, get your product into their hands, and incentivize them to corral the masses for you.

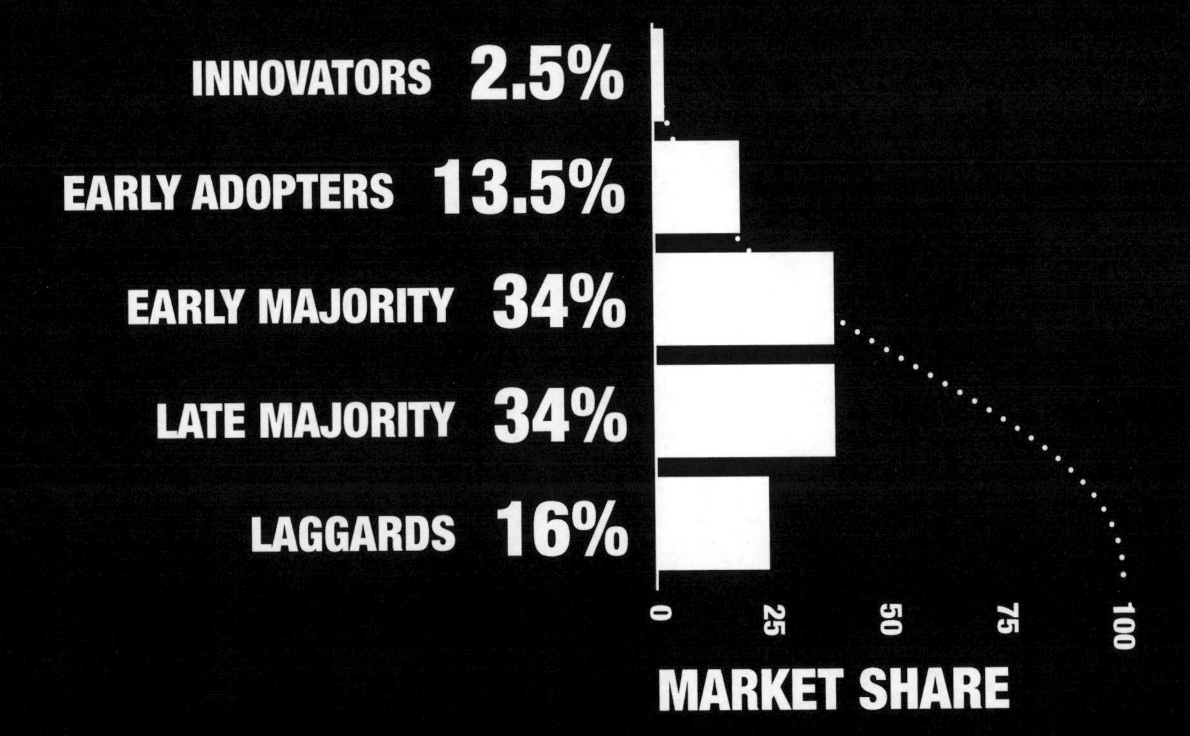
INNOVATORS 2.5%
EARLY ADOPTERS 13.5%
EARLY MAJORITY 34%
LATE MAJORITY 34%
LAGGARDS 16%
0
25
50
75
100
MARKET SHARE

The diffusion of innovations theory, made famous by Everett Rogers in his aptly titled 1962 book *Diffusion of Innovations*, simply hypothesizes that ideas are not adopted on a mass level all at once. Rather, it takes time for those ideas to spread from person to person and community to community. Makes sense, right?

As marketers, we've seen this play out in our own businesses time and time again. A small group, in this model categorized as "innovators," initially adopts the idea or product, and it gets passed from there.

While the concept appears to be common sense (and by the way, all of marketing is), it's the visualization of the concept that I find brilliant. From the curve itself, to the defined population segments, to the size of those segments, this is a step-by-step guide to sharing that even the most junior of marketers can follow.

Will this bell curve and the accompanying percentages hold true every time? No, absolutely not. But in many cases, your brand stories will spread with a similar cadence. Thanks to the bright minds who formulated this theory, we now know where and with whom to plant our seeds first.

HOMEWORK

Using your target consumer work from DARLOW Rule #32 as a starting point, identify the communities or specific individuals that fit under each of the diffusion of innovations theory's categories.

INNOVATORS (2.5%): The smallest group, these consumers are typically defined as the risk-takers within a given population. They have the highest social status and actively seek out new and often unproven ideas, beginning the word-of-mouth domino effect.

YOUR INNOVATORS: ....

....

....

....

EARLY ADOPTERS (13.5%): These thought leaders sit adjacent to the first majority group and thus are critical to the spread of an idea. While innovators may be too adventuresome for the masses, early adopters are close enough to be influential.

YOUR EARLY ADOPTERS: ....

....

....

....

EARLY MAJORITY (34%): These are the first of the mass populations to adopt an idea, but only if their thought-leading friends and family say so. While they do not often hold opinion-leader roles in a community, they are connected to those that do.

YOUR EARLY MAJORITY: ....

....

....

....

LATE MAJORITY (34%): This is a conservative population in terms of idea adoption. They'll wait for the concept to reach them, free of risk, before committing their time and/or money.

YOUR LATE MAJORITY: ....

....

....

....

LAGGARDS (16%): This is the most skeptical and reluctant of the segments. People in this group are often of lower socioeconomic status, making early adoption a financial risk. They tend to stick with what they know until they are given no other choice but to evolve.

YOUR LAGGARDS: ....

....

....

....

FISH WHERE YOUR FISH ARE

RULE #43

The next time you're being urged to buy advertising space, start by covering up the presenting media outlet's name. Instead, look only at the audience information. After all, you're not investing in the outlet; you're investing in their readership and viewership. It doesn't matter how well known the magazine or television show is; if your target consumer is not reading or watching, it's a waste of your money.

As a marketer, you should be the last person getting caught up on name brands when making buying decisions. You know better than anyone that the generic brands can often do just as well as the more expensive products you see in the commercials. Buying advertising is no different. Major television networks with name-brand programming are tempting, but if you're targeting thirteen- to seventeen-year-old aspiring comedians, a smaller, more targeted cable channel might be a better (and cheaper) fit.

People like to say "fish where the fish are"; I prefer **"fish where *your* fish are."**

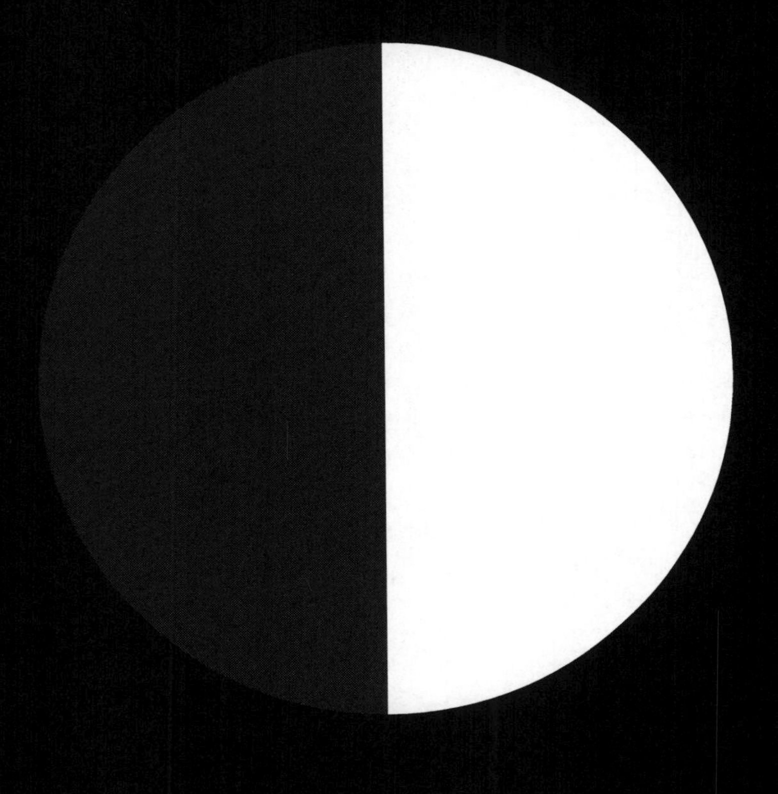

50%

IN A 2018 ARTICLE, HOOTSUITE REPORTED THAT 50% OF GEN Z (INCLUDING EIGHTEEN- AND NINETEEN-YEAR-OLDS) CONSIDERED SOCIAL MEDIA THE MOST RELEVANT CHANNEL FOR ADS. DOES THAT MATTER TO YOU?

IT DOES IF YOUR AUDIENCE IS MADE UP OF EIGHTEEN- AND NINETEEN-YEAR-OLDS.

HOMEWORK

DATE ....

Fill in the chart on the opposite page.

TARGET: These are the target consumer groups you defined in DARLOW Rule #32.

WHERE: Name where you will advertise to the target consumer group.

WHEN: State when you will advertise to the target consumer group.

ON-BRAND?: Does the media partner or outlet feed into your brand position?

TARGET	WHERE	WHEN	ON-BRAND?

HOMEWORK+12

Twelve months after you've completed your initial homework assignment on the preceding pages, come back to this rule and fill out the below to reflect your brand's current state.

DATE ....

Fill in the chart on the opposite page.

TARGET: These are the target consumer groups you defined in DARLOW Rule #32.

WHERE: Name where you will advertise to the target consumer group.

WHEN: State when you will advertise to the target consumer group.

ON-BRAND?: Does the media partner or outlet feed into your brand position?

TARGET	WHERE	WHEN	ON-BRAND?

SEEING IS BELIEVING

RULE #44

What's the difference between someone throwing up gang signs to show allegiance to a particular group and a University of Texas fan forming horns with their fingers to show allegiance to a particular school? There is no difference (and no, I'm not calling Texas fans gang members, relax).

These are simply two different paths on the way to the same destination: belonging. We all want to be part of something bigger than our individual selves. When we find our specific "tribes"—groups in which we feel embraced— we're all too willing to tell the world about our association with that gang, school, or team. Whether that means wearing a specific color or riding a particular brand of motorcycle, we become human billboards. That's where marketers like myself come in.

While a director of marketing for Adidas, I set out to create a visual that would connect our most passionate fans. Around that time, I had noticed several of my coworkers posing for pictures while holding up three fingers, representing the brand's iconic three stripes. I realized then that there was an opportunity to use a simple gesture like this to build the connection I was looking for.

Over the next few years, my team made it a point to feature our own version of that hand signal in every advertising campaign we developed. In time, it became organic. Athletes began voluntarily posting photos of themselves proudly flashing three fingers to demonstrate their loyalty to our brand. We had found a visual that united our community and proved its strength.

We knew we had a far-reaching and passionate following, but we had to prove it, and so will you. To the outside world, **seeing is believing**.

739K

IN 2015, 739,000 PEOPLE ATTENDED THE SEVENTY-FIFTH ANNIVERSARY OF THE STURGIS MOTORCYCLE RALLY IN SOUTH DAKOTA'S BLACK HILLS. WHAT DO EACH AND EVERY ONE OF THE ATTENDEES HAVE IN COMMON? LOVE FOR MOTORCYCLES. AND WHAT DO EACH AND EVERY ONE OF THE ATTENDEES DO WHEN THEY RIDE PAST A FELLOW MOTORCYCLIST? POINT TWO FINGERS TO THE GROUND IN SALUTE OF ONE ANOTHER. IT'S A SIMPLE GESTURE WITH THE POWER TO CONNECT HUNDREDS OF THOUSANDS OF PEOPLE ON A LEVEL A TELEVISION COMMERCIAL NEVER COULD.

HOMEWORK

Make a list of potential visuals you can use to connect your audiences.

OVER-SATURATION IS A GOOD THING

RULE #45

Consistency and frequency are the keys to any brand message sticking. The more times consumers hear, read, and engage with a single message, the easier it is for them to remember it. Why is it that when we see the phrase "Just Do It" we automatically think of Nike? Consistency and frequency. One slogan (consistency) since 1988 (frequency). Why is it that when we hear "Snap, Crackle, Pop!" we instantly visualize Rice Krispies? Consistency and frequency. One slogan (consistency) since 1929 (frequency).

I tell my team all the time, and now I'm telling you: **over-saturation is a good thing**. If people are tired of hearing, seeing, or reading your brand's message, you know they'll remember it, and you know you've done your job. Pick one brand message and say it over (consistency and frequency) and over (consistency and frequency) . . .

. . . and over again (consistency and frequency).

WHICH SEQUENCE IS EASIER TO REMEMBER?

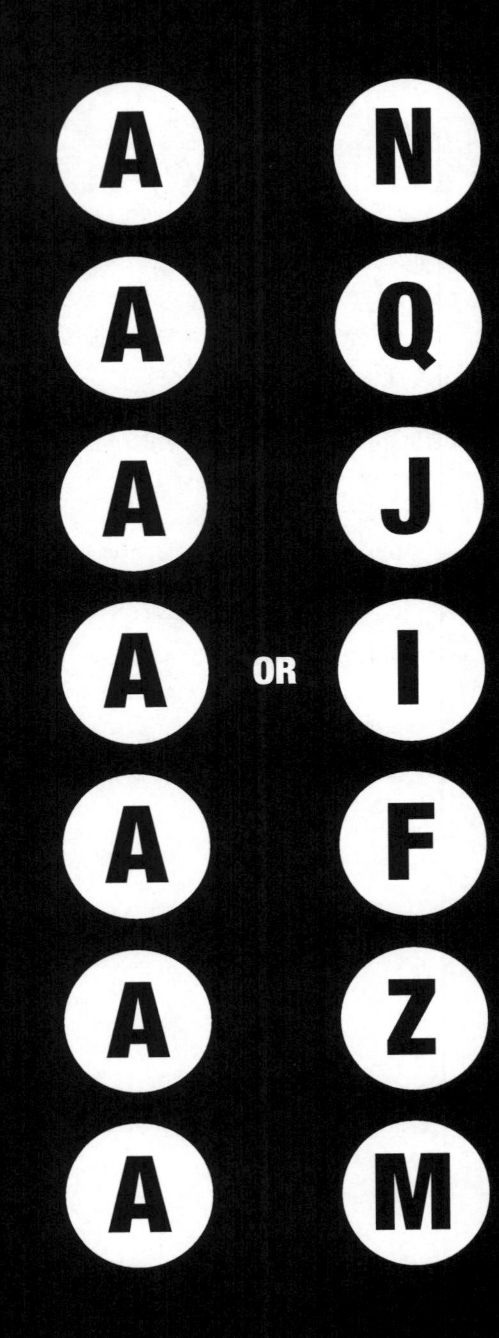

BY PRESENTING THE SAME BRAND STORY OVER AND OVER AGAIN, YOUR AUDIENCE IS MORE LIKELY TO REMEMBER YOUR MESSAGE.

HOMEWORK

DATE ....

1. Insert your positioning statement in the large circle.

2. Audit your social media by listing the subject of your last six posts to the right.

3. In the small circles, put an X next to the posts that do not reinforce your brand's positioning statement.

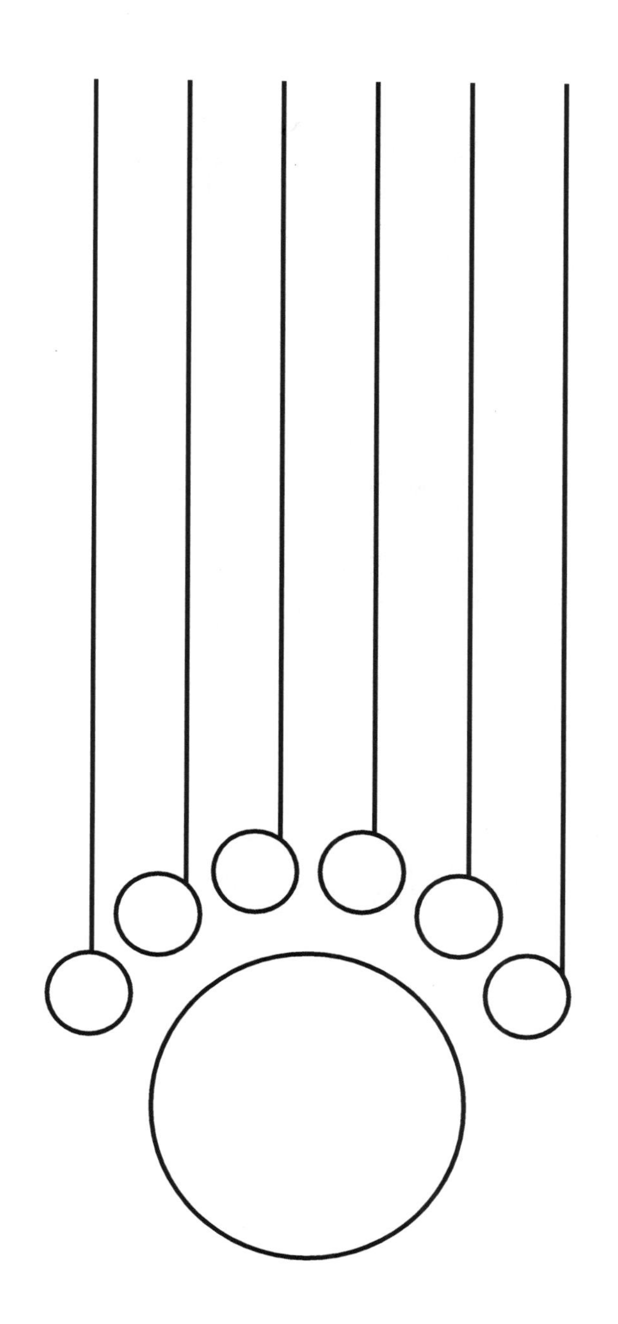

HOMEWORK+3

Three months after you've completed your initial homework assignment on the preceding pages, come back to this rule and fill out the following page to reflect your brand's current state.

DATE ....

1. Insert your positioning statement in the large circle.
2. Audit your social media by listing the subject of your last six posts to the right.
3. In the small circles, put an X next to the posts that do not reinforce your brand's positioning statement.

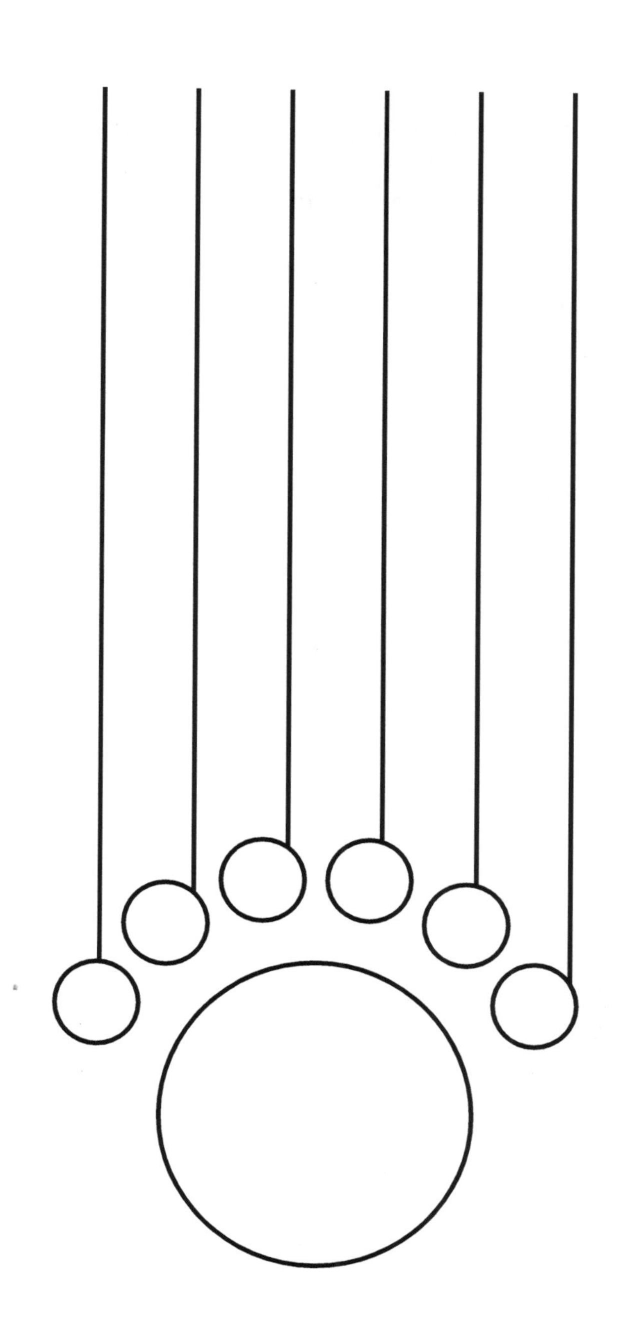

HOMEWORK+6

Six months after you've completed your HOMEWORK+3 assignment on the preceding pages, come back to this rule and fill out the following page to reflect your brand's current state.

DATE ....

1. Insert your positioning statement in the large circle.

2. Audit your social media by listing the subject of your last six posts to the right.

3. In the small circles, put an X next to the posts that do not reinforce your brand's positioning statement.

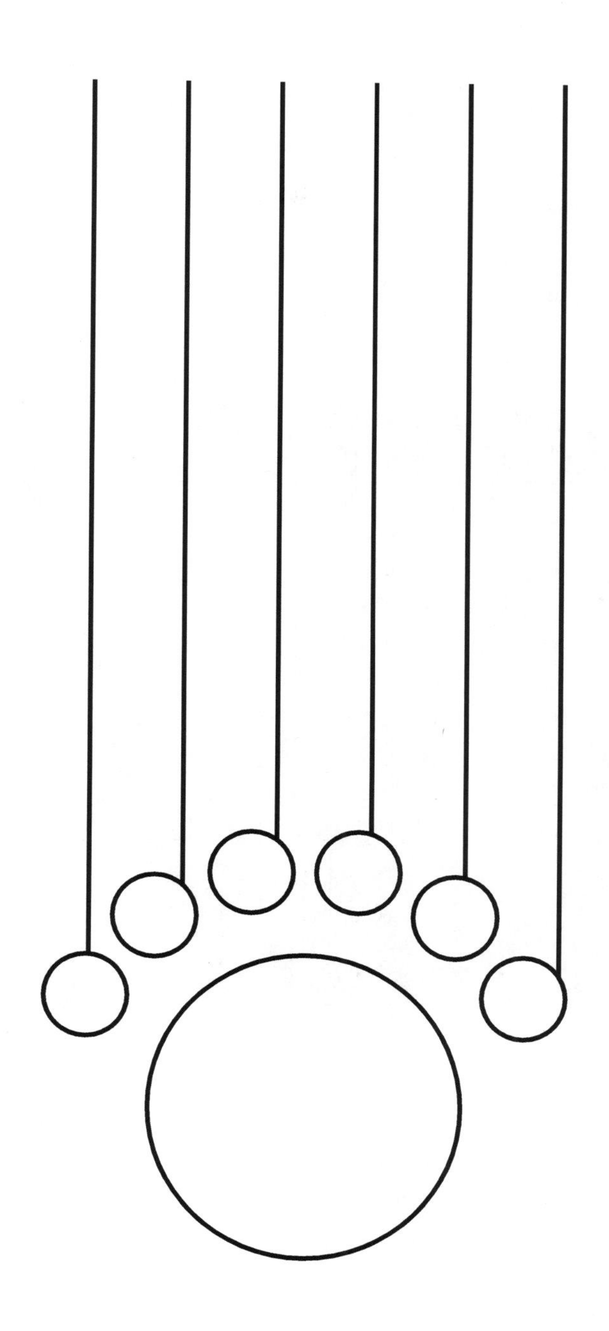

PREDICT-
ABILITY
BUILDS
TRUST

RULE #46

If people can't predict the subject of your next advertisement, you're not focused enough. While predictability may sound like a four-letter word to some creatives, as a proponent of brand consistency, I say embrace it. What those designers often fail to realize is that message stability, a marketing tenet, leads to predictability (that's the point) and that familiarity is what leads to ownership of a particular market position (that's the goal). **Predictability builds trust**, and the more that people trust your brand, the more likely they are to buy your product.

Coca-Cola has been one of the more focused and predictable brands of our time. Since introducing the "Have a Coke and a Smile" campaign in 1979, the company has made a concerted effort to regularly spread joy through its brand voice. Whether it's a tweet, a billboard, or a print campaign encouraging viewers to "Open Happiness," we know what to expect. Positivity, optimism, and a message that makes us feel good.

Similarly, Corona has carved out a niche in the beer industry through reliable messaging of its own. If I were to ask you to forecast the setting of the company's next television commercial, many of you would venture to guess "a beach." Are you a clairvoyant? No, the brand is predictable. Has that predictability, shunned by so many marketers, hurt these two brands? Hardly. In 2019 Forbes named both Coca-Cola and Corona as two of the most valuable brands in the world.

Also predictable.

WHICH FORTHCOMING SHAPE IS MORE PREDICTABLE, THAT FROM PATTERN #1 OR PATTERN #2?

PATTERN #1

PATTERN #2

HOMEWORK

DATE ....

Think of the brand activations you want to execute over the course of the next twelve months. List them in order of priority. Remember that each activation should draw from your positioning statement. If any of the below do not reinforce your position, remove them and replace them with ones that do. In this exercise, an activation can be anything that allows your brand to interact directly with your audience: for instance, an upcoming event or a seeding campaign targeting a particular consumer segment.

....

....

....

....

....

....

....

....

....

....

....

....

....

....

....

DAR
LOW

HOMEWORK+12

Twelve months after you've completed your initial homework assignment on the preceding pages, come back to this rule and fill out the below to reflect your brand's current state.

DATE ....

Make a list, in order of priority, of the brand activations you want to execute over the course of the next twelve months.

....

....

....

....

....

....

....

....

....

....

....

....

....

....

....

....

....

....

DAR
LOW

PICK ONE COLOR AND STICK WITH IT

RULE #47

In the split second that a person sees your product's packaging or advertisement, do they recognize it as yours, or do they mistake it for a competitor's product? Now, whatever you do, do not overestimate your own brand recognition. You'd be surprised at just how often people misidentify your work as someone else's.

I've been personally subjected to my share of focus group failures in which the audience confused our television spot or print ad for that of a rival. It's a painful but eye-opening experience that every young marketer should go through. Without those missteps, I may never have realized the power of color. And oh, how powerful it is.

According to a study at Loyola University Chicago, color increases brand recognition by up to 80%. Don't buy it? Let's test the theory. What color do you associate with Target department stores? Red? That's not an accident. What color comes to mind when you think of UPS? Brown? All part of the plan. How about Best Buy? Blue? Yeah, they did that on purpose too.

Before you credit their success to multimillion-dollar ad campaigns, answer two more questions. When I say "stop," what color comes to mind? And when I say "go"? (Insert lightbulb emoji.) It turns out brand associations have less to do with television commercials and more to do with regularity. You think red when I say "stop" because every time you pull up to a stop sign, it's red. Not yellow, not blue, not purple. Red. Every time.

You don't need an extravagant marketing budget to win the brand recognition battle; you just need consistency, frequency, and the self-discipline to **pick one color and stick with it**.

THE COLORS YOU CHOOSE WILL HAVE AN IMPACT ON YOUR BRAND'S PERCEPTION.

RED

PASSIONATE, BOLD, EXCITING

ORANGE

FRIENDLY, CREATIVE, ADVENTUROUS

YELLOW

OPTIMISTIC, CHEERFUL, WARM

GREEN

NATURAL, STABLE, PROSPEROUS

BLUE

TRUSTWORTHY, CALMING, DEPENDABLE

PURPLE
REGAL, WISE, SPIRITUAL

BROWN
ORGANIC, RUGGED, WHOLESOME

PINK
SENTIMENTAL, NURTURING, CARING

BLACK
SOPHISTICATED, EDGY, LUXURIOUS

WHITE
PURE, INNOCENT, VIRTUOUS

HOMEWORK

What is your brand's primary color? If you don't have one, start with your favorite color.

....

Fill in the attributes (listed on previous page) associated with that color below.

COLOR ....

....

....

....

....

....

....

....

....

....

....

....

....

....

....

....

....

....

Do these attributes fit the brand image you want to portray?

If not, find the color that does match and list it below, along with the accompanying traits.

COLOR ....

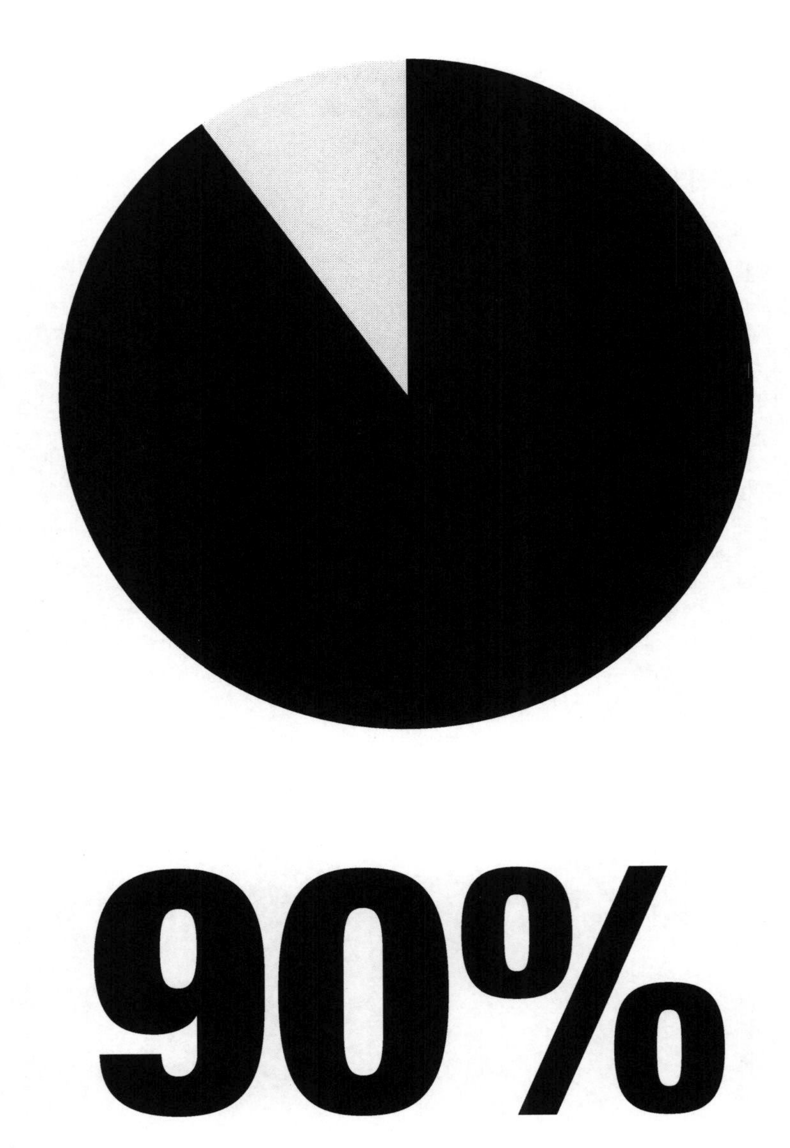
90%

ACCORDING TO RESEARCH REFERENCED BY *ENTREPRENEUR*, "UP TO 90% OF SNAP JUDGMENTS MADE ABOUT PRODUCTS CAN BE BASED ON COLOR ALONE (DEPENDING ON THE PRODUCT)."

CHOOSE WISELY.

STOP ROBBING PETER'S LOGO TO PAY PAUL

RULE #48

Let's do some (loose) math. Every time someone sees your logo, awareness and recall for that brand identifier increases. Easy, right? Okay, now here's where the arithmetic gets tricky. By adding a supplementary logo to identify that same brand, awareness and recall for that previously existing mark go down. How much they drop depends on the number of logos you bring on board and how you prioritize them.

Assuming you decide to maintain the size of your team and spread your resources equally among your newfound horde of badges, calculating that decrease is pretty straightforward. Simply divide your previously dedicated brand development time by the number of symbols now on your roster. Adding one additional mark means dividing by two. Add another, and you're forced to divide your time by three, leaving just 33% of your team's original bandwidth available per mark. The more logos you add, the less dedicated time each receives.

The math is easy, because while the number of logos available to a brand is infinite, time is not. There are twenty-four hours in a day whether you have one, two, or—lord help us—three logos. And less time devoted internally means less equity built externally. Whether you realize it or not, your new identifiers are taking away from your previous one and diluting the overall brand, not strengthening it.

So do yourself a favor and **stop robbing Peter's logo to pay Paul**.

ACCORDING TO A TWENTY-FOUR-THOUSAND-PERSON GLOBAL SURVEY DONE BY GRAPHICSPRINGS, RANKING LOGO RECOGNITION OF THE TOP TWO HUNDRED COMPANIES IN THE WORLD (BY SALES), THE MOST IDENTIFIABLE BRAND MARKS COME FROM:

COCA-COLA

FORD

SONY

APPLE

WHAT DO THESE PARTICULAR BRAND MARKS HAVE IN COMMON? CONSISTENCY AND FREQUENCY. EACH COMPANY HAS MAINTAINED A NEARLY IDENTICAL VERSION OF A SINGLE LOGO FOR DECADES.

COCA-COLA

SCRIPT SINCE 1887

FORD

BLUE OVAL SINCE 1927

SONY

TYPEFACE SINCE 1957

APPLE

ICON SINCE 1976

HOMEWORK

Draw your brand's current logo below.

Rate your logo from 1 to 10 (10 being the strongest) based on the following criteria:

RECALL: Is your logo easy to remember?
SCALE 1–10 ....

FLEXIBILITY: Does your logo work well on all advertising mediums?
SCALE 1–10 ....

STORYTELLING: Does your logo tell a brand story beyond the name?
SCALE 1–10 ....

AGELESS: Will your logo look dated in twenty years?
SCALE 1–10 ....

Taking the above criteria into account, draw a better (or first) version of your brand's logo.

ONCE IS NOT ENOUGH

RULE #49

When it comes to advertising, there is no retention without repetition. That means that single thirty-second television spot you ran during the Super Bowl probably did you no good. How do I know? A former boss told me.

Early on in my career, as I was building a paid media plan for a soon-to-launch product, my brand director advised me that anything less than three consecutive print insertions was a waste of money. The hypothesis was that it took at least three exposures to a single ad before a consumer absorbed the message. That idea stuck with me and likely kick-started my infatuation with consistency and frequency. But while my boss's experience and authority was enough to convince me, I imagine you, the reader, will want proof. And I don't blame you, so here you go.

According an article from Dartmouth College, "If one is trying to learn something well—be it a set of facts, concepts, skills, or procedures—a single exposure is usually inadequate for good long-term retention." *Time* magazine suggested as much, saying, "It's well established that repetition is key to memory," and going so far as to propose that "when you meet someone new, you might want to repeat her name thirty times." Thirty media exposures? You can't afford that; few can. But you might be able to afford to run a print ad in three consecutive issues of a magazine. Or five consecutive, or seven, or ten.

Regardless of the number, the idea is simple. The more that people see your ad, the more likely they are to remember it. And **once**, no matter how big and beautiful, **is not enough**.

10%

ACCORDING TO RESEARCH FIRM COMMUNICUS, "ONLY 10% OF CONSUMERS REMEMBER THE AVERAGE SUPER BOWL AD AND KNOW THE BRAND BEING ADVERTISED."

HOMEWORK

DATE ....

1. List any brands or products that you can recall having television commercials during last season's Super Bowl broadcast.

2. Underneath each brand, describe in a single sentence that specific commercial.

3. From there, hypothesize what the brand's communication objective was with that advertisement.

4. Of those brands and products listed, circle those that you have purchased since.

BRAND OR PRODUCT ....
COMMERCIAL DESCRIPTION ....
OBJECTIVE ....

BRAND OR PRODUCT ....
COMMERCIAL DESCRIPTION ....
OBJECTIVE ....

BRAND OR PRODUCT ....
COMMERCIAL DESCRIPTION ....
OBJECTIVE ....

BRAND OR PRODUCT ....
COMMERCIAL DESCRIPTION ....
OBJECTIVE ....

BRAND OR PRODUCT ....
COMMERCIAL DESCRIPTION ....
OBJECTIVE ....

BRAND OR PRODUCT ....
COMMERCIAL DESCRIPTION ....
OBJECTIVE ....

HOMEWORK+12

Twelve months after you've completed your initial homework assignment on the preceding pages, come back to this rule and fill out the following page to reflect your brand's current state.

DATE ....

1. List any brands or products that you can recall having television commercials during last season's Super Bowl broadcast.

2. Underneath each brand, describe in a single sentence that specific commercial.

3. From there, hypothesize what the brand's communication objective was with that advertisement.

4. Of those brands and products listed, circle those that you have purchased since.

BRAND OR PRODUCT ....
COMMERCIAL DESCRIPTION ....
OBJECTIVE ....

BRAND OR PRODUCT ....
COMMERCIAL DESCRIPTION ....
OBJECTIVE ....

BRAND OR PRODUCT ....
COMMERCIAL DESCRIPTION ....
OBJECTIVE ....

BRAND OR PRODUCT ....
COMMERCIAL DESCRIPTION ....
OBJECTIVE ....

BRAND OR PRODUCT ....
COMMERCIAL DESCRIPTION ....
OBJECTIVE ....

BRAND OR PRODUCT ....
COMMERCIAL DESCRIPTION ....
OBJECTIVE ....

SOME-
TIMES
ALL
YOU
NEED IS
A BASE
HIT

RULE #50

You're swinging the bat too hard. Brand development is about consistent base hits, not occasional grand slams. If you're managing your brand correctly, the company will enjoy a positive and steady climb to the top rather than enduring a chaotic series of highs and lows. That's exactly what you get when you try to hit a four-hundred-foot home run with every campaign.

In baseball, numbers and probability influence decision-making. If it's a tie game in the bottom of the ninth and you have the winning run on second base, you don't need a home run. **Sometimes all you need is a base hit.** Yet some people will still step up to the plate with magazine covers and highlight reels dancing in their heads and swing for the fences. Stop letting your ego lead you to irrational decision-making. A ground ball that finds a hole is the higher percentage play, takes less energy, and achieves the ultimate goal: winning.

In marketing, numbers and probability can influence your thought process in the same way—that is, if your ego allows it. Not every launch needs an expensive television campaign when alternatively investing in paid advertising on a search platform like Google can reach more people (base hit), guarantee you engagement (base hit), and cost less money (base hit).

1,421

IN 2018, THE NEW YORK YANKEES AS A TEAM BROKE THE SINGLE-SEASON HOME RUN RECORD WITH 267, WHILE AT THE SAME TIME SURPASSING THEIR OWN MARK FOR MOST STRIKEOUTS WITH 1,421.

WHETHER IT'S AMERICA'S PASTIME OR BRAND MARKETING, THE HARDER WE SWING, THE MORE WE MISS.

HOMEWORK

DATE ....

Write down the three brand objectives you listed in DARLOW Rule #24.

....

....

....

Write down the three strategies you listed in DARLOW Rule #25.

....

....

....

Now list the specific tactics you will employ in the next twelve months to carry out those strategies and ultimately reach your objectives.

HOMEWORK+12

Twelve months after you've completed your initial homework assignment on the preceding pages, come back to this rule and fill out the below to reflect your brand's current state.

DATE ....

Write down the three brand objectives you listed in DARLOW Rule #24.

....

....

....

....

....

....

....

Write down the three strategies you listed in DARLOW Rule #25.

....

....

....

....

....

....

....

....

Now list the specific tactics you will employ in the next twelve months to carry out those strategies and ultimately reach your objectives.

THERE'S MORE TO MARKET- ING THAN SOCIAL MEDIA

RULE #51

Marketers have become lazy. You're lazy. I'm lazy. We're all lazy. It's not entirely our fault. We've been brainwashed into thinking we can do everything from our computers. But we can't. **There's more to marketing than social media**, and yet that truth is being lost in the ease and convenience of Twitter, Instagram, and Facebook. If we're not careful, it's only going to get worse. Brands around the world have turned their attention to these digital platforms to the detriment of what was once called a "marketing mix."

As you've learned, ideas become sticky through consistency and frequency, meaning telling one consistent brand story and delivering that message over and over from a variety of touchpoints. The key word in this case is *variety*, something many brands lack today. If the only channel you communicate through is social media, the brand and consumer relationship becomes expected and stale. Without the help of ancillary advertising vehicles like radio, print, and out-of-home media to keep things fresh and exciting, any connection with your community is liable to wither away and ultimately die. In the same way personal trainers encourage their clients to "shock the system" by constantly changing prescribed workout routines, marketers need to relentlessly hit their audience with messages from different platforms.

If you want to build a brand people remember, log out of Instagram, step away from your desk, and engage those marketing muscles you've been ignoring.

"WITHOUT EXPERIMENTATION, A WILLINGNESS TO ASK QUESTIONS AND TRY NEW THINGS, WE SHALL SURELY BECOME

STATIC,

REPETITIVE,

MORIBUND."

—ANTHONY BOURDAIN

HOMEWORK

Approximate the number of times you have communicated through the below advertising platforms over the last twelve months.

SOCIAL MEDIA ....
TELEVISION ....
PRINT ....
OUT-OF-HOME ....
EVENTS ....
DIRECT MAIL ....
EMAIL ....
RADIO ....
ONLINE ....
OTHER ....
OTHER ....
OTHER ....

Using the template to the right, create a bar chart tracking advertising platforms (x-axis) and communication frequency among each (y-axis).

Use your largest communication number as the peak amount on the y-axis.

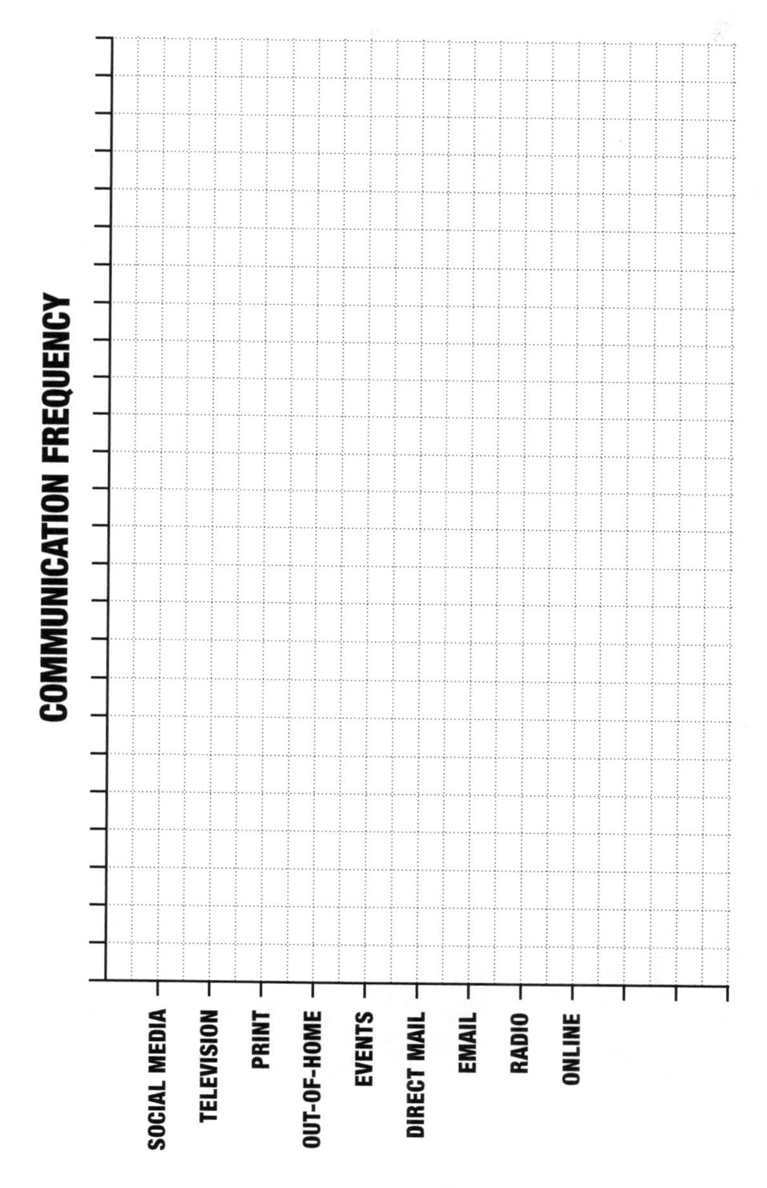
COMMUNICATION FREQUENCY
SOCIAL MEDIA
TELEVISION
PRINT
OUT-OF-HOME
EVENTS
DIRECT MAIL
EMAIL
RADIO
ONLINE
ADVERTISING PLATFORM

FAKE IT UNTIL YOUR BRAND MAKES IT

RULE #52

I've tricked you. A lot. I won't tell you in which marketing campaigns, but let me just say that I've used two tools to fool you, the audience. One is smoke, and the other is a mirror. I wielded the proverbial smoke and mirrors to dupe you into thinking the production quality of many of the brand moments I oversaw in my career were nicer than the reality. That's what you do when your budget doesn't allow for extravagance—**fake it until your brand makes it**.

Marketing magic tricks are particularly effective at company-held events, a segment of our industry that can fuel your social media feeds for weeks. But even with the content capture opportunity, there's still that pesky budget issue.

That's where the cost-conscious magician in you comes in.

First, look at the layout of your event and identify the most important physical space in terms of digital storytelling. Second, put the majority of your resources into making that particular area look phenomenal. Third, lock down your videographer and photographer on that one spot for the length of the affair. Fourth, push out your content to those following along online.

Consumers watching from home will not only regret missing out, but they'll make their disappointment known via social media. Little do they know that the sexiest part of the on-site experience is but a fraction of the actual space. And while the other parts of your event might not blow attendees away, they won't mind. Why? Because all they'll want is that single photo that carries with it social currency. And guess where they'll go to get that picture: the lovely little corner of the room where you invested all of your time and money.

Smoke, meet mirrors.

YES

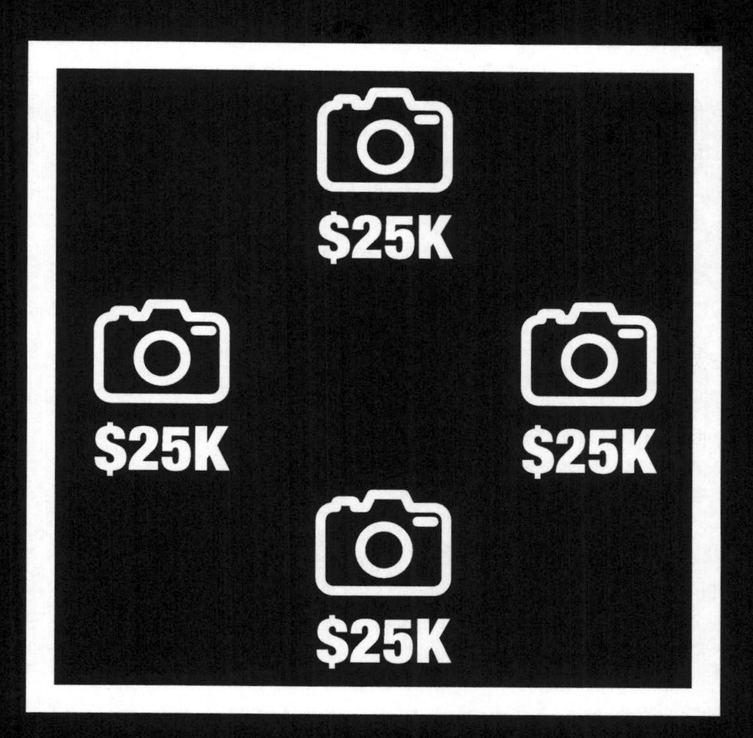

NO

HOMEWORK

Draw a rough schematic of your brand's next event floor plan.

Within that floor plan, identify the most important space for digital content capture, and draw a perimeter around that area.

Divide your production budget between that particular space and the remaining area. List the allocated dollar figures on your diagram.

Ask yourself: Are you investing in a premium destination for attendees to create and share content?

"BLACK HOLES AIN'T AS BLACK AS THEY ARE PAINTED."

—STEPHEN HAWKING

PULL
A
STUNT

RULE #53

You're in the goose bumps business, and same old, same old doesn't cut it. To make noise in today's crowded marketplace, you need to shake things up, be extraordinary, take risks, and surprise people. In other words, **pull a stunt**.

Isn't that why we got into this game in the first place? Aren't we all racking our brains to come up with the next great brand activation? Aren't we all chasing that radical new concept that lands us on *SportsCenter*, Bleacher Report, CBS Sports, *Sporting News*, *Sports Illustrated*, and Fox Sports? Well, maybe those aren't exactly your media targets, but at one point in my career, they were mine. And we got them—multiple times. How? We pulled a stunt (or four). Stunts that did shake things up, that were extraordinary, and that were risky for the brand and our careers. But they paid off in a big way.

Remember when Adidas offered the athlete who broke the forty-yard-dash record at the NFL Combine a private island? That was us. Remember when Adidas said what every Chicago Cubs fan was thinking before they won the World Series in 2016: "#$@& Curses"? That was our team too. Remember when Ellen DeGeneres took a star-studded selfie in the middle of the Oscars? That wasn't us, that was Samsung. And it was beyond brilliant. No one expected it, but everyone remembers it. You know what no one remembers from that night? The other brands that sponsored the Academy Awards. That's the point.

Marketing isn't about cookie-cutter sponsorships, logo placements, or press releases. Marketing is about crashing parties, stirring the pot, and above all else, giving people the goose bumps they deserve.

$1

BILLION

MAURICE LÉVY, CEO OF ADVERTISING FIRM PUBLICIS, ESTIMATED THE ELLEN DEGENERES OSCARS SELFIE TO BE WORTH BETWEEN $800 MILLION AND $1 BILLION.

IF THAT DOESN'T GIVE YOU GOOSE BUMPS AS A MARKETER, I DON'T KNOW WHAT WILL.

HOMEWORK

Make a list of your industry's biggest moments throughout the year.

"EITHER WRITE SOMETHING WORTH READING OR DO SOMETHING WORTH WRITING."

—BENJAMIN FRANKLIN

IT'S EASIER TO CRASH A PARTY THAN THROW A PARTY

RULE #54

Stop wasting your energy trying to bring people to your party; instead, focus on disrupting someone else's. Why? Think about it. What takes less time, money, and resources: organizing your own event or doing something disorderly at someone else's? I can tell you from experience that it's the second one. Whether it was the NFL Combine, the Great American Beer Festival, or the Electronic Entertainment Expo (known in the video game industry as E3), I learned time and time again that **it's easier to crash a party than throw a party**. To crash a party you need three things: (1) an occasion worth crashing, (2) a story to tell, and (3) influencers to tell it. Let's break each element down.

First, what do I mean by party? As it relates to your brand, a party is an event or moment of mass scale, emphasis on the words *mass scale*. If you want to make noise, you need to crash moments with the largest audiences. What is the Super Bowl of your industry? That's your party.

Second, how does one crash a party? I define *party crashing* as inserting a brand into an existing event through a disruptive and relevant activation. The focus here is on the words *disruptive* and *relevant*. If you're going to truly crash a party, you need to interrupt the regularly scheduled programming by doing something unexpected and jarring, while at the same time being authentic to your brand and pertinent to the moment.

Finally, in order for an activation to gain traction, it needs influencers backing it. Get the tastemakers within a community or industry talking about what you did, and the rest will follow.

Save yourself time, money, and resources. Stop throwing parties and instead start crashing them. It's easier that way.

BIG
PARTY

+

BOLD
STORY

+

COOL
KIDS

PARTY CRASHED

HOMEWORK

Take your industry's biggest moments from DARLOW Rule #53 and list them below, followed by ways you can crash the aforementioned moment.

MOMENT ....
IDEA ....
IDEA ....
IDEA ....
IDEA ....

MOMENT ....
IDEA ....
IDEA ....
IDEA ....
IDEA ....

MOMENT ....
IDEA ....
IDEA ....
IDEA ....
IDEA ....

MOMENT ....
IDEA ....
IDEA ....
IDEA ....
IDEA ....

MOMENT ....
IDEA ....
IDEA ....
IDEA ....
IDEA ....

MOMENT ....
IDEA ....
IDEA ....
IDEA ....
IDEA ....

MOMENT ....
IDEA ....
IDEA ....
IDEA ....
IDEA ....

MOMENT ....
IDEA ....
IDEA ....
IDEA ....
IDEA ....

DON'T CHASE THE STORM, PLAN FOR IT

RULE #55

Marketing is a lot like storm chasing: if you wait until lightning strikes to react, you're too late. The moment will have passed you by. I learned that lesson firsthand while working in sports, an industry where newsworthy headlines emerge multiple times a day, any one, two, or three of which can be leveraged by a brand. But only if you're ready.

Planning for things that haven't happened yet and may never happen is a prerequisite for the job and a lot easier than it sounds. My teams and I have faced these scenarios on countless occasions over the years. What if the Chicago Cubs win the World Series? We were ready. What if Von Miller wins NFL Rookie of the Year? We were ready. What if someone breaks the forty-yard-dash record at the NFL Combine? We were ready. And by no means is this rule exclusive to sports. What if *Assassin's Creed* (a video game brand I once worked on) reviews well? We were ready. What if Widmer Hefeweizen (a craft beer brand I once worked on) wins an award at the Great American Beer Festival? We were ready.

We had no choice, and neither do you. **Don't chase the storm; plan for it.**

Lightning is going to strike with or without you. In today's news cycle, your window to react to current events is sometimes only a few minutes long. That's plenty of time if you've been preparing for the storm to hit but no time at all if you haven't.

14.6K

During the 2013 Super Bowl, the lights went out. Literally. For over thirty minutes, the game was postponed while stadium officials tried to reverse the now infamous power outage. Naturally, people at home turned to social media in droves to respond, making it the kind of moment marketers dream of.

One brand was prepared. The team at Oreo used Twitter to insert itself into the conversation, posting a modest graphic featuring their famous cookie alone in a dimly lit room along with a caption that read, "You can still dunk in the dark." Over **14,600** retweets later, the media would proclaim Oreo as the real Super Bowl winner.

Was it luck? Nope. They were prepared. According to *Wired*, the company went into the game equipped with a fifteen-person social media team made up of copywriters and artists, each ready to react to any relevant happenings in ten minutes or less. Oreo knew lightning would strike, and when it did, they were ready.

HOMEWORK

Make a list of your industry's biggest moments from DARLOW Rule #53, followed by a brainstorm of potential occurrences that you can anticipate taking place during those events.

MOMENT ....
POTENTIAL OCCURRENCE ....
POTENTIAL OCCURRENCE ....
POTENTIAL OCCURRENCE ....
POTENTIAL OCCURRENCE ....

MOMENT ....
POTENTIAL OCCURRENCE ....
POTENTIAL OCCURRENCE ....
POTENTIAL OCCURRENCE ....
POTENTIAL OCCURRENCE ....

MOMENT ....
POTENTIAL OCCURRENCE ....
POTENTIAL OCCURRENCE ....
POTENTIAL OCCURRENCE ....
POTENTIAL OCCURRENCE ....

MOMENT ....
POTENTIAL OCCURRENCE ....
POTENTIAL OCCURRENCE ....
POTENTIAL OCCURRENCE ....
POTENTIAL OCCURRENCE ....

MOMENT ....
POTENTIAL OCCURRENCE ....
POTENTIAL OCCURRENCE ....
POTENTIAL OCCURRENCE ....
POTENTIAL OCCURRENCE ....

MOMENT ....
POTENTIAL OCCURRENCE ....
POTENTIAL OCCURRENCE ....
POTENTIAL OCCURRENCE ....
POTENTIAL OCCURRENCE ....

CONTENT IS CURRENCY

RULE #56

One thing that goes very much underutilized in the marketing world is bartering. It's a method I've employed (often by necessity based on a lack of budget) on a number of occasions, specifically in dealing with media and retailers. To each potential partner, **content is currency**, and many of you have valuable content. So stop giving it away for free.

Instead, negotiate with those targeting your audience by offering things like behind-the-scenes access, interviews with top officials, and first looks at new products. In return, ask for premium space on their sites, in their magazines, or in their stores. You get the exposure you need to build a brand, while they get the content they need to drive traffic.

“THE BEST WAY TO

LIFT

ONE’S SELF UP

IS TO

HELP

SOMEONE ELSE.”

—BOOKER T. WASHINGTON

HOMEWORK

Make a list of assets or content you would be willing to trade in return for something your brand needs (in-store exposure, advertising space, etc.).

Underneath those assets, make a list of potential trade partners along with what you would want in return from each.

CONTENT OR ASSET ....
TRADE PARTNER ....
RETURN ....
TRADE PARTNER ....
RETURN ....
TRADE PARTNER ....
RETURN ....

CONTENT OR ASSET ....
TRADE PARTNER ....
RETURN ....
TRADE PARTNER ....
RETURN ....
TRADE PARTNER ....
RETURN ....

CONTENT OR ASSET ....
TRADE PARTNER ....
RETURN ....
TRADE PARTNER ....
RETURN ....
TRADE PARTNER ....
RETURN ....

CONTENT OR ASSET ....
TRADE PARTNER ....
RETURN ....
TRADE PARTNER ....
RETURN ....
TRADE PARTNER ....
RETURN ....

CONTENT OR ASSET ....
TRADE PARTNER ....
RETURN ....
TRADE PARTNER ....
RETURN ....
TRADE PARTNER ....
RETURN ....

NO CLICKS, NO COVERAGE

RULE #57

If your brand isn't strong enough to drive traffic and sell subscriptions, the media isn't writing about you. Welcome to the digital age of journalism: **no clicks, no coverage**. But don't blame the industry, blame yourself. Before you point your fingers at the journalists, look in the mirror. Brands that have the juice are gifted with an army of publicists working on their behalf—those same reporters. Brands without are on their own. Times have changed, and so should you.

Must we celebrate the era of clickbait and breakneck reporting speeds? I won't, but I refuse to fault journalists for adapting to an industry that keeps their lights on and family fed. It's your job to recognize the motivations of the people responsible for the headlines you so desperately need. And don't get it twisted—you need them. If the media isn't writing about you, people aren't hearing about you. If people aren't hearing about you, they're certainly not following you. And if they're not following you, you're not influential.

You want headlines, they want clicks. Give the media what they want to get what you want.

58
SECONDS

ACCORDING TO *DIGIDAY*, IN 2013 THE *HUFFINGTON POST* CREATED ONE NEW ARTICLE EVERY 58 SECONDS, WHICH TRANSLATES TO BETWEEN 1,600 AND 2,000 PIECES PER DAY.

IF YOU WANT COVERAGE, THE ARTICLES ABOUT YOUR BRAND BETTER BE WORTH AN OUTLET'S (LIMITED) TIME.

HOMEWORK

Make a list of potential brand articles relevant to industry and/or national media.

INDUSTRY ARTICLES:

NATIONAL ARTICLES:

IF THEY'RE NOT FIRST, THEY'RE LAST

RULE #58

Press releases are dead, and so are the careers of the public relations directors still relying on them. As your industry evolves, so should you. If you want news coverage, put yourself in the shoes of the people writing the stories and ask, "What do *they* need to succeed?" I can tell you with certainty that they don't need another email (or attachment) to read. There's no time. Today's members of the media and the companies they work for are firmly entrenched in a battle for unique content, and the competition is fierce, not to mention vast. No longer are columnists and reporters simply battling other journos for news; thanks to social media, literally anyone with an internet connection can break a story. The pressure on these organizations is enormous; **if they're not first, they're last**.

So tell me, when are these men and women going to have time to (1) find your email, (2) open your email, and (3) read your press release? The reality is they're not. But there's another way into their hearts. Journalists are addicts too, and their drug is the exclusive. By offering a media outlet exclusive release rights to a new product unveiling, never-before-seen content, or an interview with a top executive, your chances of landing on a magazine cover or home page improve significantly.

At the end of the day, journalists have jobs they want to keep and bosses they want to make happy, just like everyone else. The better you are at helping them do those things, the more likely they are to give you the headlines you need.

345,
000,
000

A GOOGLE SEARCH OF "EXCLUSIVE"—THE MECHANISM OFTEN USED AT THE FRONT OF MEDIA HEADLINES TO SIGNAL THAT THE REPORTING ORGANIZATION HAS CONTENT NO ONE ELSE DOES—RETURNED OVER 345,000,000 NEWS RESULTS AT THE TIME OF THIS WRITING, INCLUDING STORIES FROM CNN, *VANITY FAIR*, YAHOO!, AND *USA TODAY* TO NAME A FEW.

EXCLUSIVES MATTER.

HOMEWORK

From your list of potential articles from DARLOW Rule #57, choose five of those articles and list them below along with the ideal media outlet to write that piece.

Underneath that outlet's name, list the assets or content you would be willing to provide as an exclusive and for how long.

ARTICLE ....
TARGET OUTLET ....
EXCLUSIVE ASSETS/CONTENT ....
TIMING ....

ARTICLE ....
TARGET OUTLET ....
EXCLUSIVE ASSETS/CONTENT ....
TIMING ....

ARTICLE ....
TARGET OUTLET ....
EXCLUSIVE ASSETS/CONTENT ....
TIMING ....

ARTICLE ....
TARGET OUTLET ....
EXCLUSIVE ASSETS/CONTENT ....
TIMING ....

ARTICLE ....
TARGET OUTLET ....
EXCLUSIVE ASSETS/CONTENT ....
TIMING ....

"THERE ARE ONLY TWO FORCES THAT CAN CARRY

LIGHT

TO ALL CORNERS OF THE GLOBE—THE SUN IN THE HEAVENS AND THE ASSOCIATED PRESS."

—MARK TWAIN

BREAK UP YOUR STORIES

RULE #59

When it comes to garnering headlines, size doesn't matter; length does. Public relations is no longer about generating media coverage; it's about extending and sustaining it.

The so-called twenty-four-hour news cycle continues to put pressure on reporters, keeping them on constant deadline, which means as soon as a journalist, television station, or blog has reported on your latest announcement, they're out the door chasing the next headline. Once they find it, your launch, the one you spent months building, is dead and buried, often leaving you with no more than a day of news coverage.

But there's a way to combat this harsh reality: **break up your stories**. Dissect your announcements into as many micro stories as you can without sacrificing the scale of the initial release. Brands tend to package as much content into a single announcement as possible, thinking bigger is better, when the reality is that an overstuffed media pitch leads to diminishing returns and wasted opportunities for conversation down the road. Stop scooping yourself.

Instead of releasing all of your stories on day one, hold back some of those assets and slowly push them out over the course of the next few days and weeks. By doing so, you give those coveted media outlets new reasons to continue talking about your brand.

ACCORDING TO ENCYCLOPEDIA.COM, THE ECONOMIC LAW OF DIMINISHING RETURNS IS DEFINED AS A "LAW STATING THAT IF ONE FACTOR OF PRODUCTION IS INCREASED WHILE OTHERS REMAIN CONSTANT, THE OVERALL RETURNS WILL RELATIVELY DECREASE AFTER A CERTAIN POINT." HEADLINE-SEEKING PR PROFESSIONALS AND THE BRANDS THEY SERVE CONTEND WITH THIS RULE EVERY DAY.

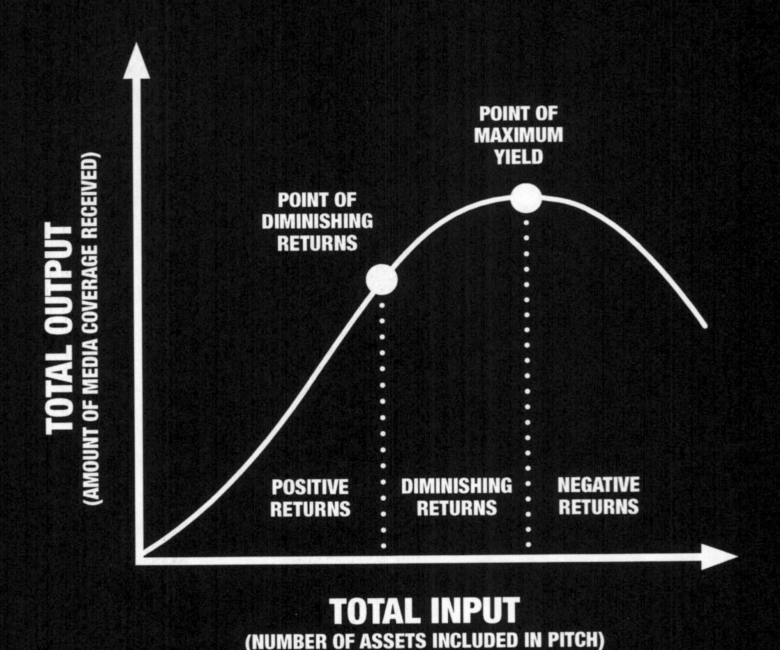

THE RELATIONSHIP BETWEEN BRANDED CONTENT AND COVERAGE IS NOT LINEAR. JUST BECAUSE YOU ADD MORE PHOTOGRAPHY OR INTERVIEWS OR BEHIND-THE-SCENES CLIPS TO YOUR DAY-ONE PRESS PACKAGE DOESN'T MEAN YOU'LL GARNER MORE HEADLINES. YOU'LL EVENTUALLY REACH A POINT OF DIMINISHING RETURNS, WHERE THE JOURNALIST GLADLY ACCEPTS YOUR CONTENT BUT REMAINS LIMITED TO THE REAL ESTATE AVAILABLE ON THE SITE THEY WRITE FOR. ADDITIONAL ASSETS AREN'T GETTING YOU A SECOND HOME PAGE HEADLINE; ALL THEY'RE GOING TO DO IS MAKE FOR A LONGER STORY.

IT'S YOUR JOB TO KNOW HOW MUCH IS TOO MUCH, THUS SAVING YOUR BRAND FROM WASTING CONTENT THAT COULD OTHERWISE BE USED TO GENERATE ADDITIONAL HEADLINES LATER IN THE YEAR.

HOMEWORK

1. Using your list of potential articles from DARLOW Rule #57, choose five of those articles and list them below along with the assets and content available from each.
2. Circle the assets or content that you plan to use as part of your announcement.
3. Next to the remaining assets or content, write the date when you plan to release that specific element.

ARTICLE ....
ASSET/CONTENT ....
ASSET/CONTENT ....
ASSET/CONTENT ....
ASSET/CONTENT ....
ASSET/CONTENT ....

ARTICLE ....
ASSET/CONTENT ....
ASSET/CONTENT ....
ASSET/CONTENT ....
ASSET/CONTENT ....
ASSET/CONTENT ....

ARTICLE ....
ASSET/CONTENT ....
ASSET/CONTENT ....
ASSET/CONTENT ....
ASSET/CONTENT ....
ASSET/CONTENT ....

ARTICLE ....
ASSET/CONTENT ....
ASSET/CONTENT ....
ASSET/CONTENT ....
ASSET/CONTENT ....
ASSET/CONTENT ....

ARTICLE ....
ASSET/CONTENT ....
ASSET/CONTENT ....
ASSET/CONTENT ....
ASSET/CONTENT ....
ASSET/CONTENT ....

FLIRT WITH YOUR AUDIENCE

RULE #60

Launching a new product or brand is a lot like courting a potential love interest. You can't ask for a person's hand in marriage the first time you meet them—well, technically you can, but this marketer doesn't recommend it. The target of your affection knows nothing about you at that point. There's still a lot of education and romancing to be done before anyone is saying "I do."

Similarly, launching a product cold turkey, minus any buildup, is just as likely to end in a no. Without any prior hype or publicity, expecting a consumer to trust that your product is worth their money is a big leap. Today nearly every commercial category looks like a dating app. We're surrounded by choices, leading people to question if your offering is right for them or if "the one" is still out there. Whether it's toothpaste or a spouse, consumers have commitment issues, so be patient with them.

When your product or brand is ready to start the wooing process, take it slow. Use the "J-curve" approach to launching a new concept (visualized on the next page). The idea is simple. Before you make your product or brand available to the public, build excitement around it first. **Flirt with your audience** in the same way you would with a prospective partner. Create a prerelease fervor so intense that when that product does go live and you are ready to ask for a shopper's (buying) commitment, they've already been begging to say "I do" for weeks.

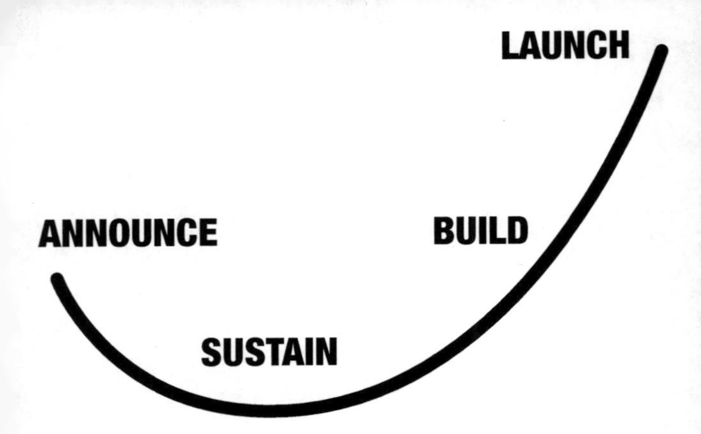

There are four phases to a successful J-curve, starting with your announcement of the product, event, endorsement, or whatever it is you want to unveil to your audience. The formula itself begins with that reveal and ends with the inevitable launch. Each is key, but it's what you do in between those two pillars that will determine your success.

Let's break each phase down.

ANNOUNCE: This is the first time your audience will have heard about your impending release; make it big and full of intrigue. In terms of timing, work back from your launch day, choosing a date that coincides with the amount of content and the number of prerelease assets you have to work with. The last thing you want is to announce so far in advance that you run out of things to say before you ever get to your launch day.

SUSTAIN: Post-announcement, your buzz will take a dip. That's okay. Your objective here is to keep the oven warm until you start ramping things back up. What you don't want to do is go cold. Continue to drop occasional nibbles of information about the impending release during this phase.

BUILD: You've kept the oven going; now it's time to turn the heat up. Steadily increase your communication frequency as you approach launch day. This is your hype phase, by the end of which every one of your consumers should be chomping at the bit to get a piece of what you have cooking.

LAUNCH: Time to pull your concept out of the oven. On this date your promotional investment and scale should peak. All hands are on deck. From public relations to paid media to social media, every cross-functional team should be focused on making launch day a success. The stronger day one is, the longer your sales, buzz, and conversation "tails" will ultimately extend. This is the moment you've been building toward.

HOMEWORK

Using your next major brand launch, fill in the date or range of dates that coincides with each phase of the J-curve.

In the space provided below each of the four phases, list the assets and content you have available to use during each period. From there, assess whether enough content exists to satisfy the needs of each phase.

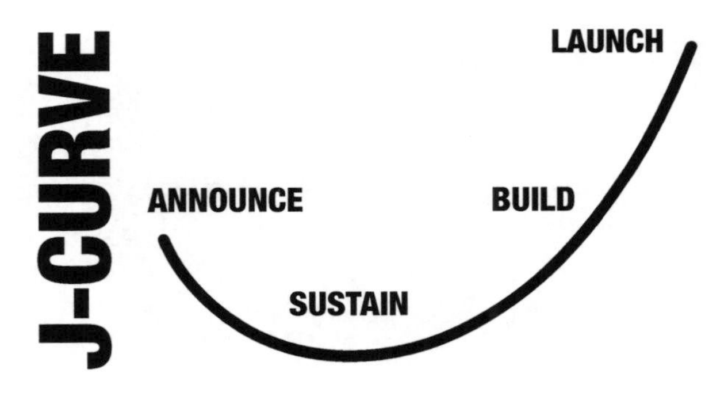

ANNOUNCE:

....

....

....

....

....

....

....

....

SUSTAIN:

BUILD:

LAUNCH:

PEOPLE WANT WHAT THEY'RE NOT SUPPOSED TO HAVE

RULE #61

Scoops sell, and they always will. Highly coveted information pays out big money and big-time social currency for those journalists, fans, and bloggers who uncover it first. Legally or illegally, these days it doesn't seem to matter. What does the next BMW look like? What does the next Oregon Ducks football uniform look like? What does the next president's tax return look like? Getting that scoop before anyone else leads to traffic, and traffic leads to fame and fortune. But what these piranhas don't realize is that we know how they're getting their news. At least sometimes we do.

While I was at one particular company, we leveraged that voracity to our advantage. Back in those days, we used something called an FTP (file transfer protocol) to share confidential files. The problem was the FTP wasn't all that secure, and people outside of our walls knew it. As a result, launch dates and future designs would often find their way onto the internet well before the company intended. Our neighborhood brand burglars got in and got out before we had a chance to react.

Until we did react—only not in the way one would expect.

Rather than further securing the FTP, we decided to occasionally leave the door unlocked. The thing about "leaked" information is that it's a lot sexier than planned news releases. **People want what they're not supposed to have**, and when they get it, they go nuts—regardless of how juicy the content is. So those rather mundane product shots we purposely planted on the FTP for our friends to steal turned a nonstory into front-page news across key blogs and news outlets throughout the industry. Free press for us and traffic for them.

Pleasure doing business with you, thieves.

"WITH GOOD ADVERTISING A GOOD PRODUCT CAN BECOME A GREAT PRODUCT."

—GEORGE LOIS

HOMEWORK

Make a list of newsworthy material or information you would be willing to leak to the media or public.

Underneath each item, make a list of target outlets or people to leak the information to.

ITEM/INFORMATION ....
TARGET OUTLET ....
TARGET OUTLET ....
TARGET OUTLET ....
TARGET OUTLET ....
TARGET OUTLET ....

ITEM/INFORMATION ....
TARGET OUTLET ....
TARGET OUTLET ....
TARGET OUTLET ....
TARGET OUTLET ....
TARGET OUTLET ....

ITEM/INFORMATION ....
TARGET OUTLET ....
TARGET OUTLET ....
TARGET OUTLET ....
TARGET OUTLET ....
TARGET OUTLET ....

RULE #62

People want fame, and brands need exposure. There's yet another deal to be done; you just need to broker it. Consumers are more than willing to act as local promoters on your behalf by helping create awareness around your latest campaign, but only if you make it worth their time. Whether it's a bit part in your next television commercial or a chance to be featured in retail stores across the country, fame is fame, and everyone wants it. I've seen that truth firsthand.

One of my earliest projects while at Adidas was a campaign that featured WNBA superstar Candace Parker. Rather than simply putting Parker's picture up in sporting goods stores, we looked for ways to involve our consumers in the campaign itself. We challenged young women from all walks of life to submit a photo montage that visualized what made them unique. The folks whose submissions received the most online votes would be featured in our campaign alongside Parker.

What transpired blew me away. By giving those who entered the contest control of the outcome, each became her own publicist. The most passionate participants rallied their schools, their friends, and their families for votes. Some even garnered local media coverage, all in an effort to win the competition. The campaign worked, and I can honestly say that the success had nothing to do with me and everything to do with today's culture. **Everyone wants their fifteen minutes of fame**, and when given the opportunity to obtain that celebrity, people will work hard for it. And for you.

1

OUT OF

9

ACCORDING TO UPROXX, "1 OUT OF 9 MILLENNIALS WOULD RATHER BE FAMOUS THAN GET MARRIED."

HOMEWORK

Make a list of exposure opportunities that you can provide to your consumers.

Underneath each opportunity, identify the target consumer group most likely to be attracted to this particular form of exposure.

EXPOSURE OPPORTUNITY ....
TARGET GROUP ....

EXPOSURE OPPORTUNITY ....
TARGET GROUP ....

EXPOSURE OPPORTUNITY ....
TARGET GROUP ....

EXPOSURE OPPORTUNITY ....
TARGET GROUP ....

EXPOSURE OPPORTUNITY ....
TARGET GROUP ....

EXPOSURE OPPORTUNITY ....
TARGET GROUP ....

EXPOSURE OPPORTUNITY ....
TARGET GROUP ....

EXPOSURE OPPORTUNITY ....
TARGET GROUP ....

EXPOSURE OPPORTUNITY ....
TARGET GROUP ....

EXPOSURE OPPORTUNITY ....
TARGET GROUP ....

EXPOSURE OPPORTUNITY ....
TARGET GROUP ....

EXPOSURE OPPORTUNITY ....
TARGET GROUP ....

EXPOSURE OPPORTUNITY ....
TARGET GROUP ....

EXPOSURE OPPORTUNITY ....
TARGET GROUP ....

EXPOSURE OPPORTUNITY ....
TARGET GROUP ....

EXPOSURE OPPORTUNITY ....
TARGET GROUP ....

EXPOSURE OPPORTUNITY ....
TARGET GROUP ....

ATTACH BRAND AND PR AT THE HIP

RULE #63

If a product launches and no one's around to hear about it, does it make a sound? In my experience, no. Great products need great brand stories, and while great brand stories come from great marketers, here's the part where even the best marketers sometimes trip up: getting the word out. Stories are only as effective as the number of people who engage with them, which is where PR comes in.

I don't care how big your advertising budget is; a well-run PR campaign is more affordable, more effective, and more believable. Whether you like it or not, the media (journalists, reporters, and bloggers) are influencers that people trust. As a result, what these entities report as news impacts our decision-making as consumers. And your PR manager is the conduit to this exceedingly persuasive community.

For that reason, if you want to be successful at building a brand, PR needs a seat at every table. **Attach your brand and PR teams at the hip**—where one goes, the other should follow. Whether that means to a meeting or an event, cover each team in Elmer's glue and stick them together. Because at the end of the day, your product launches are only as strong as the number of people who hear about them.

CONSUMER JOURNEY:

AWARENESS

CONSIDERATION

PURCHASE

AT ITS MOST BASIC, THERE ARE THREE LEVELS TO THE TRADITIONAL CONSUMER JOURNEY: AWARENESS, CONSIDERATION, AND PURCHASE, IN THAT ORDER. MEANING, BEFORE ANYONE WILL EVEN THINK ABOUT BUYING YOUR BRAND, THEY MUST FIRST RECOGNIZE THAT IT EXISTS.

AND I KNOW JUST THE TEAM TO HELP BUILD THAT AWARENESS: PR.

HOMEWORK

Look at your upcoming meeting schedule for the week. For every meeting related to brand marketing, ensure that your PR counterpart is on the invite list.

"THERE IS ONLY ONE THING IN THE WORLD WORSE THAN BEING TALKED ABOUT, AND THAT IS NOT BEING TALKED ABOUT."

—OSCAR WILDE

DON'T MAKE THE LOGO BIGGER

RULE #64

Make the logo smaller. No, seriously. In fact, remove it altogether. Logos are a crutch. Logos are lazy. And if you're doing your job right, logos are unnecessary. For decades, marketers have relied on badges to mark their territory. Whether it's a print ad, television commercial, or billboard, advertising professionals carve out as much creative real estate for their company's insignia as they can. Unfortunately that often comes at the expense of developing an easily identifiable brand look and feel. If the only way to distinguish an advertisement as yours is by an emblem, then you're doing something wrong.

Do we need a logo to identify a Picasso painting? How about a Jackson Pollock? Andy Warhol? Of course not. Despite the lack of an overpowering brand mark, we have no problem spotting Picasso's distinct cubism creations, Pollock's paint drip, and Warhol's pop art. An artist's style *is* the brand. Logo not required.

Anyone can ask for a bigger brand badge, but only a skilled marketer can develop a recognizable identity without one. The next time you review creative, ask yourself, "Would our audience be able to distinguish this work as ours without the logo?"

If not, **don't make the logo bigger**, make the brand more identifiable.

"EVERY GOOD ARTIST PAINTS WHAT HE IS."

—JACKSON POLLOCK

HOMEWORK

1. Tape your latest brand communication (print ad, social media post, product packaging, etc.) up on a wall along with the most recent examples of that variety from your competition.

2. Cover any visible logos or brand marks.

3. Poll a group of people from outside your company (ideally in your target market) and ask them to identify which brands are responsible for each piece of communication.

4. If your brand is misidentified, your look and feel is not discernable enough.

MARKET-
ING IS
EASY,
BUT
ONLY
IF YOU
ALLOW
IT TO BE

RULE #65

Marketing is easy, and yet we marketers continually make the worlds of advertising and communications more complicated than they need to be. It's more fun that way. Take taglines, for instance. At the end of the day, taglines have one purpose: to communicate to an audience what it is your company or product does. But literal language is boring to a "creative" (the communal label given to those of us who worship brainstorms, whiteboards, and desks you can write on). Instead of getting to the point, knowing full well consumers are short on time, brands often fall victim to concocting some confusing phrase that reads like an inside joke or requires a decoder ring to translate.

It's the difference between the long-standing Whole Foods Market tagline "America's Healthiest Grocery Store," which clearly identifies what makes the natural food retailer's offering unique, and the more confusing "Whatever Makes You Whole" motto the company unveiled in 2018. The former needs no further explanation, while the latter requires context, visuals, and a degree of scrutiny on the consumer's part to comprehend.

This is where a marketer's ego gets in the way. Common sense would suggest, based on society's dwindling attention span, that clear and concise phrasing makes for a better headline than catchy and clever verbiage. Common sense would also suggest that people are not buying a product because of the crafty wordplay; rather, they're buying because the product solves a need in their lives. But common sense only works if you use it. And **marketing is easy, but only if you allow it to be**.

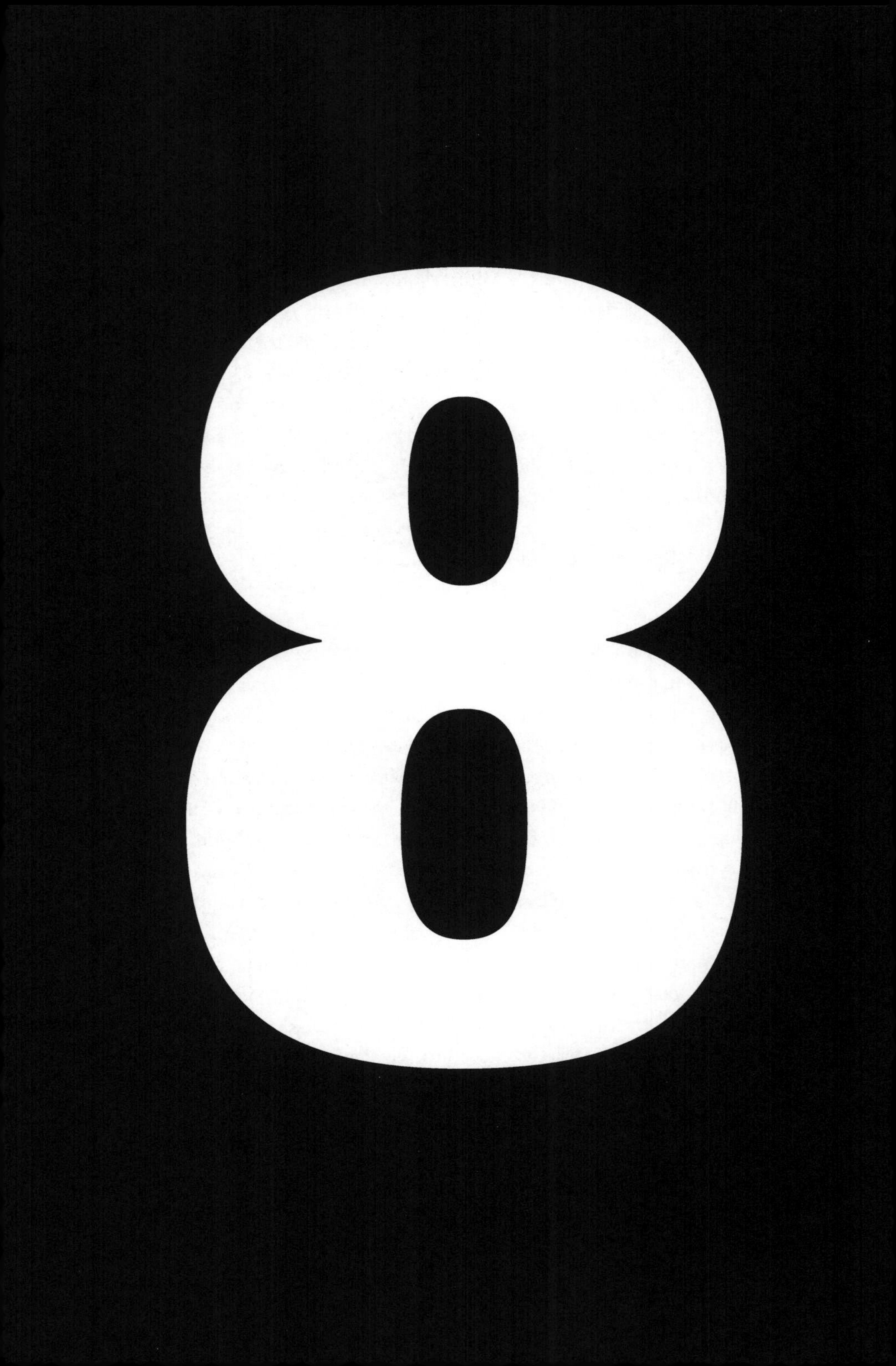
8

THE AVERAGE HUMAN ATTENTION SPAN IS 8 SECONDS, ONE SECOND LESS THAN THAT OF A GOLDFISH.

GET TO THE POINT, AND GET THERE QUICKLY.

HOMEWORK

Using five words or fewer, describe what makes your brand or product different from the competition.

....

....

....

....

....

LESS IS ALWAYS MORE

RULE #66

If you've ever suffered through a wordy PowerPoint presentation, you know how ineffective excessive verbiage can be at conveying information, especially new information. And yet, year after year, we're subjected to verbose advertising campaigns that ask too much of the consumer. In 2012, for instance, one of the world's largest fast-food chains ran a 265-word print ad to (comedically) defend one of its key ingredients. For context, the DARLOW Rule that you're reading right now is just 223 words. It's yet another example of marketers failing to use their own life experiences (and common sense) to inform their work.

If full sentences are overwhelming for someone stuck in a boardroom with nowhere else to look but at the screen, why then would a similarly wordy approach work for consumers casually flipping through a lobby magazine? It doesn't. In fact, overcommunicating never works. Not in a boardroom, not in a lobby, not even on a computer. As advertising goes, **less is always more**.

According to an article in *Marketing Week*, just 9% of digital ads are viewed for more than one second. One second! The majority of consumers are barely scanning your ads, which means the more copy you're packing into them, the less likely shoppers are to read them. Anything over a few words and you're just wasting banner space, budget, and time.

“PERFECTION

IS FINALLY ATTAINED NOT WHEN
THERE IS NO LONGER ANYTHING
TO ADD, BUT WHEN THERE IS
NO LONGER ANYTHING TO

TAKE AWAY.”

—ANTOINE DE SAINT-EXUPÉRY

HOMEWORK

Using three words or fewer, describe what makes your brand or product different from the competition.

....

....

....

Could this be your new tagline?

BIG AND BOLD IS BETTER THAN BOLD AND BEAUTIFUL

RULE #67

If your audience is to remember one thing from your next advertisement, what do you want it to be? Picture it. Whether "it" is a product shot, a celebrity endorser, or a tagline, imagine the element in your head. Got it? Okay, now when you're ready to build this particular ad, make sure "it" is big. Really big. Bigger than anything else on the page, screen, or billboard. As I used to say to my design agency partners, if it's important to the campaign, "I want to see it from space." And you should too.

When designing two-dimensional promotional vehicles like print ads, billboards, and even websites, size matters. A static image is only as good as the creative's ability to stop people, and scale is a tool marketers can use to draw an audience in. That's step one, two, and three. Yes, it's that important.

If your creative doesn't get the reader to pause and examine your ad, it's a failure, no matter how pretty it is. When it comes to capturing attention, **big and bold is better than bold and beautiful**.

x

X

WHICH X DREW YOUR EYE FIRST?

IN DESIGN TERMS, VISUAL WEIGHT IS A MEASURE OF HOW MUCH SOMETHING ATTRACTS THE EYE. AS IT RELATES TO SIZE, LARGER OBJECTS TEND TO APPEAR HEAVIER THAN SMALLER OBJECTS, WHICH IS WHY MOST OF YOU SAW THE BIGGER X ON THE RIGHT FIRST. AND WHILE SIZE IS NOT THE ONLY DETERMINANT ON WHERE THE EYE'S GAZE WILL GO, IT'S A FACTOR—ONE YOU CAN AND SHOULD USE TO YOUR ADVANTAGE IN YOUR MARKETING MATERIALS.

HOMEWORK

1. Review your latest visual advertisement (print ad, billboard, Instagram photo, etc.).

2. What brand message did you intend for your audience to take away from this particular piece of collateral?

3. List in order the specific visual elements within the imagery that draw your eye first, second, and third.

VISUAL ....

VISUAL ....

VISUAL ....

Does the order in which the imagery draws your eye align with the intended consumer takeaway?

If the order in which your eye is drawn does not match your own messaging priorities, make a note and fix it on your next creative execution.

NO ONE CARES WHO DID IT FIRST

RULE #68

Wait, you're telling me your brand was the first to post on Twitter? Before anyone else?!

No one cares.

No seriously—no one cares. Not even you. Can you name the first brand to develop a print ad? How about a billboard? Okay, let's use a more modern example. Which brand had the first Facebook page? Not sure? Neither am I. In advertising, no one cares who got there first. In our industry, there's no such thing as a "first-mover advantage." Instead, credit goes to those who are patient.

Rather than racing to the next hot social media platform or marketing trend, take a beat and assess whether that space makes sense for your brand in the first place. Fit will ultimately determine your success, not expedience. While you're doing your due diligence, those competitors who sprinted to the starting line will iron out the technology's wrinkles for you. As first movers spend precious time and energy stumbling through foreign territory, smart brands watch and wait because **no one cares who did it first**. What matters is who does it best.

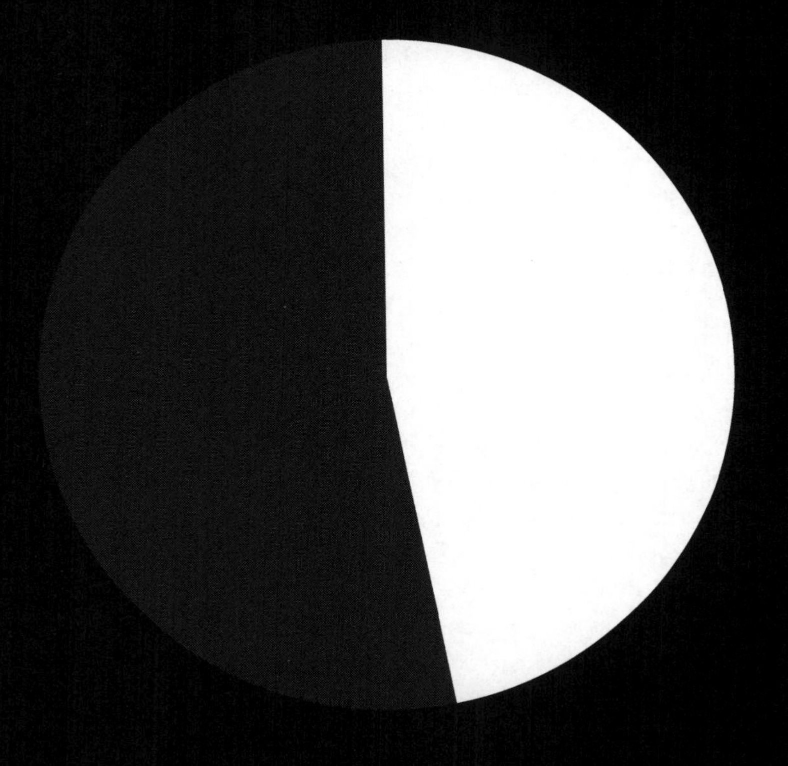

47%

ACCORDING TO AMERICAN PSYCHOLOGIST AND UNIVERSITY OF PENNSYLVANIA PROFESSOR ADAM GRANT, 47% OF FIRST-MOVER COMPANIES FAIL IN THEIR EARLY YEARS COMPARED TO JUST 8% OF SO-CALLED IMPROVERS, WHO WERE NOT FIRST BUT ENHANCED THE ORIGINAL CONCEPT.

HOMEWORK

Name (without looking them up) the first brands to execute or participate in the below advertising platforms (write your answers next to each).

TELEVISION COMMERCIALS ....
PRINT ADVERTISING ....
OUT-OF-HOME ADVERTISING ....
RADIO ADVERTISING ....
FACEBOOK ....
TWITTER ....
INSTAGRAM ....

Chances are, you didn't name many.

Now name the companies you think do the best job at executing or participating in the below advertising platforms today (write your answers next to each).

TELEVISION COMMERCIALS ....
PRINT ADVERTISING ....
OUT-OF-HOME ADVERTISING ....
RADIO ADVERTISING ....
FACEBOOK ....
TWITTER ....
INSTAGRAM ....

I'm willing to bet you had more success coming up with brands for this exercise than the previous one. That's because we remember the best in class, not the first to arrive.

DON'T BE AFRAID TO COPY, JUST MAKE IT BETTER

RULE #69

Another former boss (I've had my share) once gave me advice that changed the way I view competition. He said, **"Don't be afraid to copy, just make it better."** If you're going to emulate another brand's concept or activation, improve upon it. That's advice I took to heart and have used to my advantage ever since. The truth of the matter is that there are no original ideas nowadays. Too many marketers and too many brands exist in the world for a 100% unique concept to spawn. Whether you realize it or not, what you see, read, and hear every day has influenced you. And that's okay. What's not okay is to live by the expectation that your next promotion is going to be one of a kind. That's a waste of time and energy, neither of which I can afford to squander, so I don't.

If you were to check my Google search history, you would find plenty of queries for phrases like "most disruptive marketing campaigns" and "best advertising stunts of the year." Do I reproduce the exact concepts I find without making adjustments to them? No. But am I constantly looking for inspiration and motivation? Absolutely. If someone else successfully executed a campaign that can benefit my brand, you better believe I'm co-opting it. You should too.

"WHEN THERE'S ANYTHING TO STEAL,

I STEAL."

—PICASSO

HOMEWORK

1. Google the phrase "best advertising stunts of (insert year)."
2. From the results, make a list of your favorite stunts and why you like them.
3. Circle those executions your brand can steal.

STUNT ....
WHY ....
WHY ....
WHY ....

STUNT ....
WHY ....
WHY ....
WHY ....

STUNT ....
WHY ....
WHY ....
WHY ....

STUNT ....
WHY ....
WHY ....
WHY ....

STUNT

WHY

WHY

WHY

STUNT

WHY

WHY

WHY

STUNT

WHY

WHY

WHY

STUNT

WHY

WHY

WHY

STUNT

WHY

WHY

WHY

STUNT

WHY

WHY

WHY

DON'T JUST MAKE IT BETTER, MAKE IT YOURS

RULE #70

Let's be honest: if the idea is obvious to you, it's probably obvious to your competition. That means stopping at that initial light-bulb moment is a formula for sameness. So don't stop. Instead, take the thought and continue tweaking. Create a version specific to your brand and your brand alone. Find the angle only you can speak to with authority. Do that. **Don't just make it better, make it yours.**

In simple terms, create an original remix of an unoriginal concept. The more you realize that's all any of us are doing (knowingly or unknowingly remixing previously executed ideas), the more unique your version of marketing will be.

“ORIGINALITY
IS THE ART OF
CONCEALING
YOUR SOURCES.”

—FRANKLIN P. JONES

HOMEWORK

Take the advertising stunts from DARLOW Rule #69 and list them below, followed by ways in which your brand can remix those ideas and turn them into your own original concepts.

STUNT ....

....

HOW TO MAKE IT YOURS ....

....

....

....

....

STUNT ....

....

HOW TO MAKE IT YOURS ....

....

....

....

....

STUNT ....

....

HOW TO MAKE IT YOURS ....

....

....

....

STUNT

HOW TO MAKE IT YOURS

STUNT

HOW TO MAKE IT YOURS

STUNT

HOW TO MAKE IT YOURS

STUNT

HOW TO MAKE IT YOURS

IF YOU'RE GOING TO SAY IT, SAY IT WITH CONFI-DENCE

RULE #71

A former colleague of mine once said, "If you say it with confidence, it's true." A frightening but accurate statement nonetheless. On the whole, humans are not good at detecting lies. In fact, according to NBC News, research suggests that people are able to distinguish truths from deceits just 53% of the time. Add confidence to the equation, and it gets even more complicated. An article from *Psychology Today* submits, "[Overconfidence] has a knack for seducing people to such a degree that they *ignore* the results." Self-assurance is potent—and a little scary.

Let me be clear: I am not suggesting you lie. In fact, I strongly advocate against it. Not only is it just plain wrong, but your brand will ultimately face severe consequences when (not if) those fabrications are discovered.

Rather than looking at this rule pessimistically, let's take it in from another angle. If conviction can lead a falsehood to be seen as a truth, then a lack of conviction can turn a truth into a falsehood. *Psychology Today* also suggests that "people who don't believe in themselves—whether that belief is well-grounded or not—aren't likely to convince others to buy in." Brands are no different. If you're not delivering a message with unwavering faith, you're putting yourself at risk. How many consumers are willing to take a chance with their hard-earned money on a brand that doesn't seem to be confident in its own product? Not many.

Like it or not, my former colleague was right. **If you're going to say it, say it with confidence.**

“I AM THE GREATEST,

I SAID THAT EVEN BEFORE I KNEW I WAS.”

—MUHAMMAD ALI

HOMEWORK

DATE ....

On a scale of 1 to 10, how confident is your brand voice?

Make it a goal to improve this number over the coming months.

HOMEWORK+3

Three months after you've completed your initial homework assignment on the preceding pages, come back to this rule and fill out the below to reflect your brand's current state.

DATE ....

On a scale of 1 to 10, how confident is your brand voice?

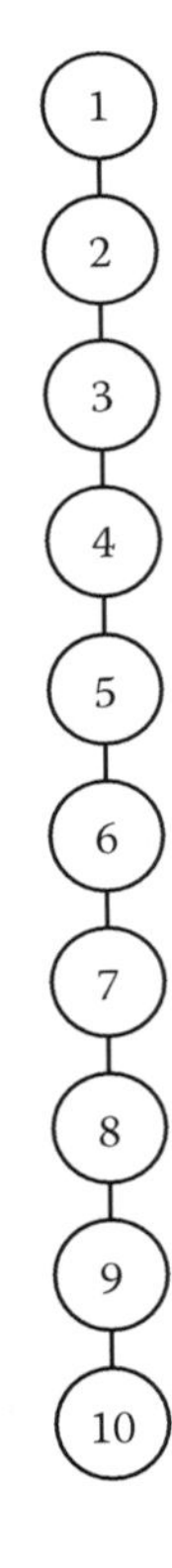

Make it a goal to improve this number over the coming months.

HOMEWORK+6

Six months after you've completed your HOMEWORK+3 assignment on the preceding pages, come back to this rule and fill out the below to reflect your brand's current state.

DATE ....

On a scale of 1 to 10, how confident is your brand voice?

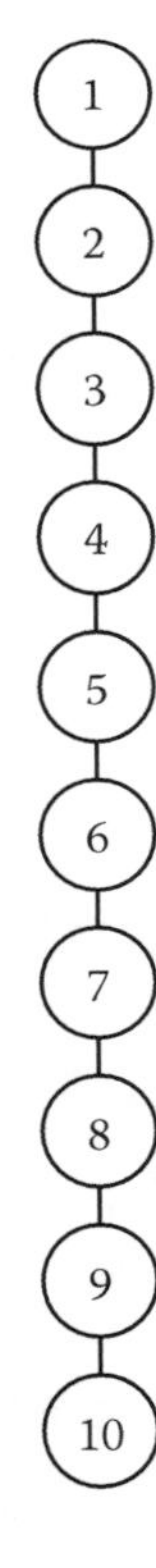

Make it a goal to improve this number over the coming months.

DON'T BRAND SCARED

RULE #72

How do you build a confident brand? Give it license to fail. I've yet to work with a company that didn't pass on an opportunity out of fear of something going wrong. I've yet to meet a person completely free of insecurity or anxiety. But what if we, as marketers, weren't afraid? How would our brands look? Act? Talk? The answer is, different, stronger, and with more self-assuredness.

Over my career and life, I've had certain wisdom from people I admire permanently burned into my mind. One of those messages that I'll always carry with me is this: "Don't live scared." But we do. We all do. We're scared of the unknown. Of trying new things. Of taking risks. Unfortunately those also happen to be surefire tendencies that can kill a brand.

Marketing isn't black or white. There's no right or wrong answer. Sometimes things work to perfection, but more often than not, they don't. It's that expectation of perfection that equates to a marketer's kryptonite. Perfection creates bland, safe, and lifeless marketing. Perfection breeds the insecurity, anxiety, and apprehension we're surrounded by every day. And ultimately, chasing perfection can kill brands.

Rather than letting fear of failure destroy your brand's confidence, take the advice of my former colleague, with a marketing twist: **don't brand scared**.

"NOT FAILURE, BUT LOW AIM IS THE CRIME."

—BRUCE LEE

HOMEWORK

Make a list of ways you would promote your brand if there were no consequences, followed by what you perceive to be the potential risks of those promotions.

PROMOTION ....
RISKS ....
RISKS ....
RISKS ....

PROMOTION ....
RISKS ....
RISKS ....
RISKS ....

PROMOTION ....
RISKS ....
RISKS ....
RISKS ....

PROMOTION ....
RISKS ....
RISKS ....
RISKS ....

PROMOTION ....

RISKS ....

RISKS ....

RISKS ....

PROMOTION ....

RISKS ....

RISKS ....

RISKS ....

PROMOTION ....

RISKS ....

RISKS ....

RISKS ....

PROMOTION ....

RISKS ....

RISKS ....

RISKS ....

PROMOTION ....

RISKS ....

RISKS ....

RISKS ....

PROMOTION ....

RISKS ....

RISKS ....

RISKS ....

CARPE DIEM

RULE #73

What are you waiting for? Are you waiting for new business to come to you without any encouragement? Are you assuming the competition is simply going to concede on their own? I can promise you that neither is going to happen. In fact, while you're sitting back and relaxing, your rivals are more than likely stealing the existing market share you worked so hard to earn. Sadly, you're not alone.

It happens every day. Brands wait too long to strike. Rather than overinvesting when things are going well and the competition is vulnerable, many do the exact opposite, waiting to put dollars and resources toward marketing until their own company is struggling. What keeps these brands from capitalizing on success? Greed and arrogance.

When corporations are ascending, they can often become intoxicated by today's revenue. The goal shifts from long-term brand development to short-term profit gain. Rather than pressing down on the pedal, the conservative companies take their foot off the gas and spend less. Instead of stepping on the competition's throat, the overconfident ones let their rivals up off the canvas and wait for their response. That's when the opposition knocks them on their asses.

You don't get many chances to **seize the day** as a brand. When one presents itself, take advantage.

$2

BILLION

PER STATISTA, NETFLIX INCREASED ITS MEMBERSHIP FROM APPROXIMATELY 21 MILLION SUBSCRIBERS IN 2011 TO OVER 54 MILLION BY THE END OF 2017. YET DESPITE THAT ASTOUNDING GROWTH, THE COMPANY REFUSED TO PULL BACK. IT OPTED INSTEAD TO INCREASE ITS MARKETING BUDGET, PER CNBC, FROM $1.28 BILLION IN 2017 TO A MASSIVE $2 BILLION IN 2018. WHEN THE IRON WAS HOT, NETFLIX CHOSE TO STRIKE.

WHAT WOULD YOU CHOOSE?

HOMEWORK

DATE ....

Write down the areas in which your brand is excelling.

Underneath each, list the ways in which you are bringing attention to that specific triumph.

WIN ....
STRATEGY ....
STRATEGY ....
STRATEGY ....
STRATEGY ....
STRATEGY ....

WIN ....
STRATEGY ....
STRATEGY ....
STRATEGY ....
STRATEGY ....
STRATEGY ....

WIN ....
STRATEGY ....
STRATEGY ....
STRATEGY ....
STRATEGY ....
STRATEGY ....

Now ask yourself, can you be doing more?

HOMEWORK+3

Three months after you've completed your initial homework assignment on the preceding pages, come back to this rule and fill out the below to reflect your brand's current state.

DATE ....

Write down the areas in which your brand is excelling.

Underneath each, list the ways in which you are bringing attention to that specific triumph.

WIN ....
STRATEGY ....
STRATEGY ....
STRATEGY ....
STRATEGY ....

WIN ....
STRATEGY ....
STRATEGY ....
STRATEGY ....
STRATEGY ....

WIN ....
STRATEGY ....
STRATEGY ....
STRATEGY ....
STRATEGY ....

Now ask yourself, can you be doing more?

HOMEWORK+6

Six months after you've completed your HOMEWORK+3 assignment on the preceding pages, come back to this rule and fill out the below to reflect your brand's current state.

DATE ....

Write down the areas in which your brand is excelling.

Underneath each, list the ways in which you are bringing attention to that specific triumph.

WIN ....
STRATEGY ....
STRATEGY ....
STRATEGY ....
STRATEGY ....

WIN ....
STRATEGY ....
STRATEGY ....
STRATEGY ....
STRATEGY ....

WIN ....
STRATEGY ....
STRATEGY ....
STRATEGY ....
STRATEGY ....

Now ask yourself, can you be doing more?

"THERE ARE RISKS AND COSTS TO A PROGRAM OF ACTION. BUT THEY ARE FAR LESS THAN THE LONG-RANGE RISKS AND COSTS OF COMFORTABLE INACTION."

—JOHN F. KENNEDY

BREAK THE RULES

RULE #74

Rules are to a marketer as blood is to a great white shark. Once we get a whiff of an arbitrary law, we race to attack it. When someone says, "That's how we've always done it," all we hear is a dinner bell. That's because rule breaking drives conversation, and brands worth talking about are brands worth buying.

When Elvis shook his hips and offended thousands along the way, it got people talking. He won. When Joe Namath wore white cleats among a sea of black cleats, breaking the league's uniform policy, it got people talking. He won. When the Detroit police stormed the stage during an N.W.A. concert in 1989, preventing the group from playing one of their "controversial" songs, it got people talking. The band won.

If you want to get journalists and social media buzzing, **break the rules**. Get in your car and drive the wrong way down a one-way brand street. It's worth the ticket.

$10,326

$3,213

ACCORDING TO A 2011 ARTICLE BY CBS NEWS, MEN WHO WERE DEEMED "AGREEABLE" MADE $10,326 LESS PER YEAR THAN MEN CONSIDERED "A BIT DIFFICULT," WHILE AGREEABLE WOMEN MADE $3,213 LESS ANNUALLY.

IT TURNS OUT FOLLOWING THE RULES DOESN'T GET PEOPLE TALKING OR PAID.

HOMEWORK

Make a list of industry-relevant rules that your brand can and would be willing to break, followed by ways in which you could break them.

RULE TO BREAK ....
HOW ....

....

RULE TO BREAK ....
HOW ....

....

RULE TO BREAK ....
HOW ....

....

RULE TO BREAK ....
HOW ....

....

RULE TO BREAK ....
HOW ....

....

RULE TO BREAK ....
HOW ....

....

RULE TO BREAK ....
HOW ....

....

RULE TO BREAK ....
HOW ....

....

RULE TO BREAK ....
HOW ....

....

RULE TO BREAK ....
HOW ....

....

RULE TO BREAK ....
HOW ....

....

RULE TO BREAK ....
HOW ....

....

RULE TO BREAK ....
HOW ....

RULE TO BREAK ....
HOW ....

....

"IN ORDER TO BE A PERFECT MEMBER OF A FLOCK OF SHEEP, ONE HAS TO BE, FOREMOST, A SHEEP."

—ALBERT EINSTEIN

REWRITE THE RULES

RULE #75

This is it. You've reached the last rule. There's not much left to say, except to ask that you don't listen to me. Unless you want to. But please forget everything you just read. Unless you agree with it. This book is not an attempt to brainwash; it's an attempt to teach and inspire a new generation of marketer. That's you. What you take away, what you believe, and what you do from here is up to you.

But do something.

Do not leave this experience and simply file it away with the rest of our industry's rhetoric. Come back again and again, each time improving upon the plan we've built together over the course of seventy-five rules. Continue to take action—your action, not mine. Not Seth Godin's. Not Malcolm Gladwell's. Yours. There are enough sheep masquerading as marketers in our world today who are pushing out the same boring content year after year. That's not you. You're different. You wouldn't have bought this book if the fire to leave a legacy didn't burn inside of you. You wouldn't have made it this far if not for an urge to create, to disrupt, and to innovate. You can be the next Godin or Gladwell or Darlow, but don't. Be the next you.

Starting now.

In the introduction of this book, I challenged you to take in the forthcoming pages with intention. To trash the rules you hate, steal the rules you love, and build from there. That time has come. It's your turn to craft an original legacy. It's your turn to build a one-of-a-kind brand. It's your turn to **rewrite the rules**.

Your rules, not mine.

HOMEWORK

1. Make a list of the DARLOW Rules you agree with and plan to carry out in your own marketing plans going forward.
2. Add to this list the rules you have adopted from other marketing books (reference your work in DARLOW Rule #2).
3. Finally, add to this list your own personal rules on brand marketing.

RULE ....
RULE ....
RULE ....
RULE ....
RULE ....
RULE ....
RULE ....
RULE ....
RULE ....
RULE ....
RULE ....
RULE ....
RULE ....
RULE ....
RULE ....
RULE ....
RULE ....
RULE ....

RULE ....
RULE ....
RULE ....
RULE ....
RULE ....
RULE ....
RULE ....
RULE ....
RULE ....
RULE ....
RULE ....
RULE ....
RULE ....
RULE ....
RULE ....
RULE ....
RULE ....
RULE ....
RULE ....
RULE ....
RULE ....
RULE ....
RULE ....
RULE ....

And with that, I introduce to you

THE .... **RULES.**
(INSERT YOUR NAME)

FINAL WORDS

Every year I go on a solo trip (yes, just me—no friends, no companions, just me). My travels have taken me to places like Yellowstone National Park, London, Bangkok, the Grand Canyon, and my all-time favorite, Byron Bay in Australia. Why do I do it? To challenge myself? Learn about myself? Scare myself? I suppose it's some combination of the three, with each trip bringing a different recipe and mixture. As I write these final words, I'm in the midst of my latest pilgrimage, a road trip from Portland, Oregon, to Banff National Park in Alberta, Canada. Each voyage is different and the same. No matter where I end up or what I do while I'm there, I always leave stronger, more capable, and more confident.

As I sit here, journaling to you from a coffee shop in Idaho on my way home from this latest mission, I'm wishing the same experience for you as you read this book. The cover has my name on it, but the pages are more yours than they are mine. I realized on this trip that every book we read is a personal quest in itself. We start in the same place, but how we get to the last page is never replicated. Each knowledge journey is special.

I hope that as you read this book, you felt challenged, you learned about yourself, and you scared yourself. I hope that as you come to the end of this experience, you feel stronger, more capable and confident. But most of all, I hope you feel empowered to do something great. To use your education for good. We need you.

Calling on all marketers: You are some of the most powerful people in our world because you understand us better than anyone else does. You know how to change our minds, shape our opinions, and convince us to take action. You have the ability to make our planet a better place.

But none of that matters unless you take action first, unless you fight the urge to put this book on your shelf next to the other paperback trophies you've conquered over the years. Leave it in your bag, keep it on your desk, let it continually breathe life into you. Let it be a reminder of what you're capable of. Let it take you to a place only you can go.

MARKETING

DATE: ....

BRAND: ....

POSITIONING STATEMENT: (From Rule #18 homework)

....

....

CONSUMERS: (From Rule #32 homework)

1. ....
2. ....
3. ....

OBJECTIVES: (From Rule #24 homework)

1. ....
2. ....
3. ....

STRATEGIES: (From Rule #25 homework)

1. ....
2. ....
3. ....

PLAN

TACTICS: (From Rule #50 homework)

1. ....

2. ....

3. ....

4. ....

5. ....

6. ....

7. ....

8. ....

9. ....

10. ....

11. ....

12. ....

MARKETING

DATE: ....

BRAND: ....

POSITIONING STATEMENT: (From Rule #18 homework)

....

....

CONSUMERS: (From Rule #32 homework)

1. ....

2. ....

3. ....

OBJECTIVES: (From Rule #24 homework)

1. ....

2. ....

3. ....

STRATEGIES: (From Rule #25 homework)

1. ....

2. ....

3. ....

PLAN

TACTICS: (From Rule #50 homework)

1. ....

2. ....

3. ....

4. ....

5. ....

6. ....

7. ....

8. ....

9. ....

10. ....

11. ....

12. ....

MARKETING

DATE: ....

BRAND: ....

POSITIONING STATEMENT: (From Rule #18 homework)

....

....

CONSUMERS: (From Rule #32 homework)

1. ....

2. ....

3. ....

OBJECTIVES: (From Rule #24 homework)

1. ....

2. ....

3. ....

STRATEGIES: (From Rule #25 homework)

1. ....

2. ....

3. ....

PLAN

TACTICS: (From Rule #50 homework)

1. ....

2. ....

3. ....

4. ....

5. ....

6. ....

7. ....

8. ....

9. ....

10. ....

11. ....

12. ....

BIBLIOGRAPHY

Abadi, Mark, and Allana Akhtar. "Mark Cuban Just Revealed He Has Nearly $1 Billion in Amazon Stock. Here Are All the Ways the 'Shark Tank' Investor Made and Spends His $4.1 Billion Fortune." *Business Insider*, October 1, 2019. https://www.businessinsider.com/mark-cuban-net-worth-2018-9.

Ahmad, Irfan. "The Rising Importance of Influencer Marketing—Statistics and Trends." Social Media Today, March 18, 2018. https://www.socialmediatoday.com/news/the-rising-importance-of-influencer-marketing-statistics-and-trends-info/519084/.

Andrews, Robert. *The Columbia Dictionary of Quotations*. New York: Columbia University Press, 1993.

Baer, Drake. "9 Books Billionaire Warren Buffett Thinks Everyone Should Read." *Business Insider*, September 2, 2014. https://www.businessinsider.com/warren-buffett-favorite-business-books-2014-8.

Basketball Reference. "NBA & ABA Career Leaders and Records for Total Rebounds." Accessed June 17, 2019. https://www.basketball-reference.com/leaders/trb_career.html.

Baseball Reference. "New York Yankees Team Yearly Batting Stats." Accessed June 25, 2019. https://www.baseball-reference.com/teams/NYY/batteam.shtml.

Battan, Carrie. "Ellen DeGeneres and the Trap of Trying to Be 'Relatable.'" *New Yorker*, January 7, 2019. https://www.newyorker.com/culture/culture-desk/ellen-degeneres-and-the-trap-of-trying-to-be-relatable.

Bedbury, Scott. *A New Brand World: 8 Principles for Achieving Brand Leadership in the 21st Century*. New York: Viking, 2002.

Binet, Les, and Peter Field. *The Long and Short of It: Balancing Short- and Long-Term Marketing Strategies*. London: IPA, 2013.

Bloem, Craig. "84 Percent of People Trust Online Reviews as Much as Friends. Here's How to Manage What They See." *Inc.*, July 31, 2017. https://www.inc.com/craig-bloem/84-percent-of-people-trust-online-reviews-as-much-.html.

Boeck, Scott. "2018 MLB Season: 13 Statistics to Sum It Up, from Strikeouts to Home Runs." *USA Today*, October 2, 2018. https://www.usatoday.com/story/sports/mlb/2018/10/02/mlb-season-home-runs-strikeouts/1449184002/.

Bonhote, Ian, director. Peter Ettedgui, writer. *McQueen*. Bleecker Street, 2018.

Bourdain, Anthony. *Medium Raw: A Bloody Valentine to the World of Food and the People Who Cook*. New York: Ecco Press, 2010.

Burton, David L. "Diffusion Theory." University of Missouri Extension, accessed June 24, 2019. http://extension.missouri.edu/greene/documents/ACHTworkshop/Diffusion.pdf.

Butler, Andy. “Interview with Art Director George Lois.” Designboom, July 10, 2014. https://www.designboom.com/design/interview-with-art-director-george-lois-07-10-2014/.

Calaprice, Alice, ed. *The New Quotable Einstein.* Princeton, NJ: Princeton University Press, 2005.

Cassidy, Peter. “Survey Finds Consumers Crave Authenticity—and User-Generated Content Delivers.” Social Media Today, November 21, 2017. https://www.socialmediatoday.com/news/survey-finds-consumers-crave-authenticity-and-user-generated-content-deli/511360/.

Clarke, Nikki. “Budgeting for the Upturn—Does Share of Voice Matter.” Nielsen, August 6, 2009. https://www.nielsen.com/us/en/insights/news/2009/budgeting-for-the-upturn-does-share-of-voice-matter.html.

Communicus. “The $10 Million Minute: 80% of Super Bowl Ads Fail, Reveals Communicus.” Press release, February 3, 2017. https://www.communicus.com/2017/02/03/10-million-minute-80-super-bowl-ads-fail-reveals-communicus/.

Cooper, Paige. “Social Media Advertising Stats That Matter to Marketers in 2018.” Hootsuite, June 5, 2018. https://blog.hootsuite.com/social-media-advertising-stats/.

Couric, Katie. “Exclusive: Ruth Bader Ginsburg on Hobby Lobby Dissent.” Yahoo! News, July 30, 2014. https://www.yahoo.com/news/katie-couric-interviews-ruth-bader-ginsburg-185027624.html.

Denys, Patti, and Mary Holmes. *Animal Magnetism: At Home with Celebrities and Their Animal Companions*. Darby, PA: Diane Publishing Co., 1998.

DiSalvo, David. "The Surprising, Infuriating Power of Overconfidence." *Psychology Today*, October 15, 2014. https://www.psychologytoday.com/us/blog/neuronarrative/201410/the-surprising-infuriating-power-overconfidence?amp.

Dockterman, Eliana. "Read the Full Transcript of *Master of None* Writer Lena Waithe's Moving Emmys Speech." *Time*, September 18, 2017. https://time.com/4945661/lena-waithe-emmys-speech-master-of-none/.

Douglas, Scott. "To Run Faster, Get a Rival." *Runner's World*, July 8, 2014. https://www.runnersworld.com/training/a20794869/to-run-faster-get-a-rival/.

Fiegerman, Seth. "Analyst: iPhone Launch Attracts Longest Line Ever at Apple Flagship Store." Mashable, September 20, 2013. https://mashable.com/2013/09/20/apple-iphone-lines/#2eWTdp25vmq0.

Forbes. "The World's Most Valuable Brands." 2019 ranking. https://www.forbes.com/powerful-brands/list/2/#tab:rank.

Forde, Pat. "Appalachian State Earns Role as Conquering Hero." ESPN, September 1, 2007. https://www.espn.com/espn/columns/story?columnist=forde_pat&id=3001214&sportCat=ncf.

Frank, Leonard Roy. *Random House Webster's Quotationary*. New York: Random House, 1999.

Fullerton, Laurie. "Online Reviews Impact Purchasing Decisions for Over 93 Percent of Consumers, Report

Suggests." The Drum, March 27, 2017. https://www.thedrum.com/news/2017/03/27/online-reviews-impact-purchasing-decisions-over-93-consumers-report-suggests.

Gallo, Amy. "The Value of Keeping the Right Customers." *Harvard Business Review*, October 29, 2014. https://hbr.org/2014/10/the-value-of-keeping-the-right-customers.

Gilmore, Mikal. "Tom Petty's Real-Life Nightmares: Rocker on *Damn the Torpedoes* Woes." *Rolling Stone*, February 21, 1980. https://www.rollingstone.com/music/music-features/tom-pettys-real-life-nightmares-rocker-on-damn-the-torpedoes-woes-116826/.

Gilot, Françoise, and Carlton Lake. *Life with Picasso*. New York: McGraw-Hill, 1964.

Godin, Seth. "Nothing." *Seth's Blog*, March 13, 2009. https://seths.blog/2009/03/nothing/.

———. *Purple Cow: Transform Your Business by Being Remarkable*. New York: Portfolio, 2003.

Google Dictionary. "Echo Chamber." Accessed June 13, 2019. https://www.google.com/search?q=Dictionary#dobs=echo%20chamber.

Grant, Adam. "The Surprising Habits of Original Thinkers." Filmed February 2016. TED video, 15:17. https://www.ted.com/talks/adam_grant_the_surprising_habits_of_original_thinkers#t-143796.

GraphicSprings. "Most Powerful Logo Survey." Accessed June 25, 2019. https://www.graphicsprings.com/most-powerful-logos.

Haedrich, Marcel. *Coco Chanel: Her Life, Her Secrets.* New York: Robert Hale, 1972.

Hagel, John, Maggie Wooll, John Seely Brown, and Alok Ranjan. "If You Love Them, Set Them Free." Deloitte, June 6, 2017. https://www2.deloitte.com/insights/us/en/topics/talent/future-workforce-engagement-in-the-workplace.html.

Hagy, Jessica. "Sun Tzu's *The Art of War*, Illustrated (Chapter 7: Maneuvering)." *Forbes*, October 22, 2013. https://www.forbes.com/sites/jessicahagy/2013/10/22/sun-tzus-the-art-of-war-illustrated-chapter-7-maneuvering/#3bb1587562d2.

Handly, Lucy. "Netflix Just Increased Its Marketing Budget to $2 Billion. Here's Why Its CEO Would Rather Not Spend Anything." CNBC, updated February 8, 2018. https://www.cnbc.com/2018/01/23/netflix-2018-marketing-budget-to-hit-2-billion.html.

Harris Interactive. "Just Google Me: How Our Personal Search Results Affect Our Everyday Relationships, from Who We Do Business With, Who We Vote For, and Even Who We Date." Brand Yourself, 2012. https://brandyourself.com/blog/wp-content/uploads/harris-study.pdf.

Hawking, Stephen. "Black Holes Ain't as Black as They Are Painted." Reith Lectures 2015, BBC Radio 4 transcript. http://downloads.bbc.co.uk/radio4/transcripts/2015_Reith_Lecture_Hawking_ep2.pdf.

Hotz, Tyler. "Unthinkable Upset Yields Unthinkable Impact Ten Years After App-Michigan." *The Appalachian*, August 30, 2017. https://theappalachianonline.com

/unthinkable-upset-yields-unthinkable-impact-10-years-app-michigan/.

Housel, Morgan. "The Peculiar Habits of Successful People." *USA Today*, August 24, 2014. https://www.usatoday.com/story/money/personalfinance/2014/08/24/peculiar-habits-of-successful-people/14447531/.

Jobs, Steve. "The Seed of Apple's Innovation." Bloomberg, October 11, 2004. https://www.bloomberg.com/news/articles/2004-10-11/the-seed-of-apples-innovation.

Johnson, Robert, and Eric Goldschein. "17 Everyday Facts You Know Are Correct—That Are Totally Wrong." *Business Insider*, November 9, 2011. https://www.businessinsider.com/15-everyday-facts-that-are-totally-wrong-2011-8.

Jones, Jonathan. "Britain's Best-Loved Artwork Is a Banksy. That's Proof of Our Stupidity." *The Guardian*, July 26, 2017. https://www.theguardian.com/commentisfree/2017/jul/26/britain-artwork-banksy-art-girl-with-balloon.

Kang, Sean H. K. "Spaced Repetition Promotes Efficient and Effective Learning: Policy Implications for Instruction." *Policy Insights from the Behavioral and Brain Sciences* 3, no. 1 (2016): 12–19. doi: https://doi.org/10.1177/2372732215624708.

Kee, K. F. "Adoption and Diffusion." In *International Encyclopedia of Organizational Communication*, edited by C. Scott and L. Lewis. Hoboken, NJ: Wiley-Blackwell, 2017.

Kelly, Christina. "Kurt and Courtney Sitting in a Tree." *Sassy*, April 1992.
Kilpatrick, Andrew. *Of Permanent Value: The Story of Warren Buffett*. Birmingham, AL: 8th Avenue Books, 2006.
Labrecque, Lauren, and George R. Milne. "To Be or Not to Be Different: Explorations of Norms and Benefits of Color Differentiation in the Marketplace." *Marketing Letters* 24, no. 2 (June 2013). doi: https://doi.org/10.1007/s11002-012-9210-5.
Linkner, Josh. "Banksy's Shredded Painting Was a Moment of Creative Brilliance." *Detroit Free Press*, October 13, 2018. https://www.freep.com/story/money/business/columnists/josh-linkner/2018/10/13/banksy-shredder-business/1614965002/.
Little, John, ed. *Striking Thoughts: Bruce Lee's Wisdom for Daily Living*. North Clarendon, VT: Tuttle Publishing, 2000.
Lorimer, George. *Letters from a Self-Made Merchant to His Son*. Boston: Small, Maynard, 1904.
Love, Alaina. "Leadership, Passion, and the Presidency." *Harvard Business Review*, October 28, 2008. https://hbr.org/2008/10/leadership-passion-and-the-pre.html.
Marden, Orison Swett. *How They Succeeded*. Interview with Alexander Graham Bell. Boston: Lothrop, 1901.
Marx, Groucho. *Groucho and Me*. New York: Bernard Geis Associates, 1959.
Matthews, Gail. "The Effectiveness of Four Coaching Techniques in Enhancing Goal Achievement: Writing Goals, Formulating Action Steps, Making a Commitment, and Accountability." Presented

at the Ninth Annual International Conference on Psychology, Athens, Greece, May 25–28, 2015. https://www.atiner.gr/abstracts/2015ABST-PSY.pdf.

Mautz, Scott. "Do You Fear Criticism? Science Explains Why (and Gives These Six Fixes)." *Inc.*, November 28, 2017. https://www.inc.com/scott-mautz/science-says-were-wired-to-fear-criticism-so-fix-it-with-these-6-tips.html.

May, Cindi. "Most People Consider Themselves to Be Morally Superior." *Scientific American*, January 31, 2017. https://www.scientificamerican.com/article/most-people-consider-themselves-to-be-morally-superior/.

McGinn, Daniel. "Life's Work: An Interview with Jerry Seinfeld." *Harvard Business Review*, January–February 2017. https://hbr.org/2017/01/lifes-work-jerry-seinfeld.

McSpadden, Kevin. "You Now Have a Shorter Attention Span Than a Goldfish." *Time*, May 14, 2015. https://time.com/3858309/attention-spans-goldfish/.

Moline, Peg. "We're Far More Afraid of Failure Than Ghosts: Here's How to Stare It Down." *Los Angeles Times*, October 31, 2015. https://www.latimes.com/health/la-he-scared-20151031-story.html.

Mooney, Phil. "A Coke and a Smile." Coca-Colacompany.com, August 4, 2008. https://www.coca-colacompany.com/stories/a-coke-and-a-sm.

NBA Encyclopedia. "Classic NBA Quotes: Magic and Larry." Accessed June 21, 2019. http://archive.nba.com/history/Classic_NBA_Quotes_Magic_and_Larry.html.

NBC News. "Ellen's Oscar Selfie: Worth $1 Billion?" April 9, 2014. https://www.nbcnews.com/tech/social-media/ellens-oscar-selfie-worth-1-billion-n75821.
New America. "Perception vs. Reality: The Typical College Student." Accessed June 17, 2019. https://www.newamerica.org/in-depth/varying-degrees/perception-vs-reality-typical-college-student/.
News-Sentinel (Lodi, CA). "Times Call for Liberal Action, Says Kennedy." May 13, 1961.
Nolan, Ali. "The Steve Prefontaine Interview You Probably Haven't Seen Before." *Runner's World*, September 28, 2016. https://www.runnersworld.com/runners-stories/g20823687/the-steve-prefontaine-interview-you-probably-havent-seen-before/.
Nudd, Tim. "Angry Cheeseburger Defends Itself in 265-Word McDonald's Ad." *AdWeek*, September 13, 2012. https://www.adweek.com/creativity/angry-cheeseburger-defends-itself-265-word-mcdonalds-print-ad-143663/.
Oaklander, Mandy. "5 Best Ways to Improve Your Memory." *Time*, September 29, 2015. https://time.com/4042569/how-to-improve-memory/.
O'Reilly, Lara. "11 Things Hardly Anyone Knows About Nike." *Business Insider*, November 5, 2014. https://www.businessinsider.com.au/history-of-nike-facts-about-its-50th-anniversary-2014-11.
Osburn, Christopher. "New Data Reveals Just How Desperately Millennials Want to Be Famous." Uproxx, January 25, 2017. https://uproxx.com/life/millennials-desperately-want-to-be-famous/.

Perrin, Andrew. "Who Doesn't Read Books in America?" Pew Research Center, March 23, 2018. https://www.pewresearch.org/fact-tank/2018/03/23/who-doesnt-read-books-in-america/.

Petronzio, Matt. "Only 2% of People Can Multitask Successfully." Mashable, August 13, 2012. https://mashable.com/2012/08/13/multitasking-infographic/#OSFQK7Obv5qq.

Rapinoe, Megan. "Dear Megan: A Letter to My Thirteen-Year-Old Self." Bleacher Report, August 5, 2016. https://thelab.bleacherreport.com/dear-megan/.

Reston, James. "Beware the Fury of a Patient Man." *New York Times*, July 1, 1960. https://www.nytimes.com/1960/07/01/archives/beware-the-fury-of-a-patient-man.html.

Rice Krispies history page, accessed June 25, 2019. https://www.ricekrispies.com/en_US/snap-crackle-pop.html.

Ries, Al, and Jack Trout. *Positioning: The Battle for Your Mind*. New York: McGraw-Hill, 1981.

Rodman, Selden. *Conversations with Artists*. Interview with Jackson Pollock. New York: Capricorn Books, 1961.

Rowling, J. K. "The Fringe Benefits of Failure and the Importance of Imagination." Commencement Address, Annual Meeting of the Harvard Alumni Association, June 2008. https://harvardmagazine.com/2008/06/the-fringe-benefits-failure-the-importance-imagination.

Saint-Exupéry, Antoine de. *Wind, Sand, and Stars*. New York: Reynal and Hitchcock, 1939.

Schmid, Gretchen. "Business Statistics: 19 Essential Numbers to Know in 2019." Fundera, June 14, 2019. https://www.fundera.com/blog/small-business-statistics.

Sculley, John, with John A. Byrne. *Odyssey: Pepsi to Apple—A Journey of Adventure, Ideas, and the Future*. New York: Harper & Row, 1987.

Seave, Ava. "Fast Followers Not First Movers Are the Real Winners." *Forbes*, October 14, 2014. https://www.forbes.com/sites/avaseave/2014/10/14/fast-followers-not-first-movers-are-the-real-winners/#7566457e314c.

Shepherd, Maddie. "Keep Your Customers Coming Back: 13 Brand Loyalty Statistics You Need to Know." Fundera, updated July 23, 2019. https://www.fundera.com/resources/brand-loyalty-statistics.

Singh, Satyendra. "Impact of Color on Marketing." *Management Decision* 44, no. 6 (2006): 783–89. doi: https://doi.org/10.1108/00251740610673332.

Sreenivasan, Sree. "How Googling Others Affects Voting, Hiring, and Dating." CNET, October 14, 2012. https://www.cnet.com/news/how-googling-others-affects-voting-hiring-and-dating/.

Staples, Andy. "The Greatest Upset of Them All." *Sports Illustrated*, accessed June 21, 2019. https://www.si.com/longform/appstate/index.html.

Statista. "Apple's Revenue Worldwide from 2004 to 2018 (in Billion US Dollars)." November 6, 2018. https://www.statista.com/statistics/265125/total-net-sales-of-apple-since-2004/.

———. "Attitudes Towards Marketing Content Personalization in the United States as of April 2017."

February 20, 2018. https://www.statista.com/statistics/808313/personalization-marketing-perspectives/.

———. "Number of Netflix Paying Streaming Subscribers in the United States from 3rd Quarter 2011 to 3rd Quarter 2019 (in Millions)." Accessed June 27, 2019. https://www.statista.com/statistics/250937/quarterly-number-of-netflix-streaming-subscribers-in-the-us/.

Steinhilber, Brianna. "How to Tell If Someone Is Lying to You." NBC News, August 15, 2017. https://www.nbcnews.com/better/health/how-tell-if-someone-lying-according-behavioral-experts-ncna786326.

Sternberg, Josh. "10 Lessons for Brands from the Huffington Post." Digiday, March 19, 2013. https://digiday.com/media/the-huffpo-way/.

Sullivan, Bob, and Hugh Thompson. "Brain, Interrupted." *New York Times*, May 3, 2013. https://www.nytimes.com/2013/05/05/opinion/sunday/a-focus-on-distraction.html.

Urban Dictionary. "Cool by Association." Accessed June 24, 2019. https://www.urbandictionary.com/define.php?term=cool%20by%20association.

US News & World Report. "Nearly Half a Million People Attend Sturgis Motorcycle Rally." October 12, 2018. https://www.usnews.com/news/best-states/south-dakota/articles/2018-10-12/nearly-half-a-million-people-attend-sturgis-motorcycle-rally.

Walsh, Fiona. "Indian-Born Nooyi Takes Over at PepsiCo." *The Guardian*, August 14, 2006. https://

www.theguardian.com/business/2006/aug/15
/genderissues.uknews.

Washington, Booker T. *The Story of My Life and Work.* New York: J. L. Nichols, 1901.

Watercutter, Angela. "How Oreo Won the Marketing Super Bowl with a Timely Blackout Ad on Twitter." *Wired*, February 4, 2013. https://www.wired.com/2013/02/oreo-twitter-super-bowl/.

Weisul, Kimberly. "It Doesn't Pay to Be Nice. This Is How Much It Costs." CBS News, updated August 7, 2011. https://www.cbsnews.com/news/it-doesnt-pay-to-be-nice-this-is-how-much-it-costs/.

Wilde, Oscar. *Lady Windermere's Fan* in *The Importance of Being Earnest and Other Plays.* London: Penguin, 1940.

World Bank. Total population. Accessed June 18, 2019. https://data.worldbank.org/indicator/SP.POP.TOTL.

NOTES

NOTES

NOTES